Stephen Hill comes with a true prophetic voice that sharply divides between soul and spirit. He shares with absolute authenticity, bringing together a rich theological perspective developed over many years, combined with his own personal experience and the realities of his own human struggle. In his search for the true nature and intent of God he has come to understand firsthand the insights that he shares in this book

- DENISE JORDAN - FOUNDER AND DIRECTOR OF
FATHERHEART MINISTRIES

In his book, 'Freedom From Religion', Stephen comes with a cutting prophetic voice and powerful Biblical clarity to restore the truth of the gospel, at a time when the Church is being challenged with greater perspectives of God our Father and His place in our Christian experience. I highly recommend this book for all who endeavour to have a vital part in the ongoing growth and health of the Body of Christ in the future

- JAMES JORDAN - FOUNDER AND DIRECTOR OF
FATHERHEART MINISTRIES

FREEDOM *from* RELIGION

Stephen Hill

PREVIOUSLY PUBLISHED AS 'PRIMAL HOPE'

©2024

Freedom From Religion - by Stephen Hill
Published by Fatherheart Ministries 2024

Second edition by Stephen Hill - Ancient Future 2019
First edition published in 2016 with the title:
Primal Hope - Finding Confidence Beyond Religion

Cover & Layout by Tom Carroll

ISBN: 978-0-473-46787-6

All scripture quotations, unless otherwise indicated, are taken from the English Standard Version® (ESV®). All rights reserved.

Freedom From Religion is available from Amazon.com in Paperback and Kindle formats and at www.fatherheart.net/store

I wish to acknowledge the invaluable contributions of my wife, Becky, as well as Alice Adams and Tom Carroll in helping prepare this book for publication.

To James and Denise Jordan

Contents

Introduction

*"But whatever gain I had...I count as rubbish,
that I may gain Christ and be found in Him, not
having a righteousness of my own."*

- Philippians 3:7,8

In 2008, my life passed through a watershed that can only be described as remarkable. What happened then put my Christianity into perspective and brought a resolution of my life as a human being with faith in God. This occurred at the very edge of the world for me. Being a man from Belfast, I couldn't have gone any further. I ended up on a remote island off the coast of Auckland, New Zealand where I spent three months in beautiful yet spartan surroundings, in the company of fifty others from different nations. I was at a residential school called *Inheriting the Nations* organised by Fatherheart Ministries. What happened there was nothing less than a seismic shift in my worldview, a turning inside out of the fabric of spirituality that had appeared to be a mature Spirit-filled walk with God. It was a homecoming at levels much deeper than my comprehension. In short, everything changed. I knew what it was to be truly born again, to start anew from the beginning.

When I landed on Great Barrier Island, my mature and well-established Christianity was in ruins. The rubble of my faith lay around my feet. My head was full of knowledge but my heart was empty. Experientially, I had become an unbeliever. As far as an inner experience of the peace and love of God in my heart went, I had nothing more than someone who did not believe in any god or have any spirituality. I had been brought up in the Exclusive Brethren with a comprehensive knowledge of the Bible. Within the Charismatic Movement I had received the baptism of the Spirit, spoken in tongues and moved powerfully in spiritual gifts. I had spent my life up to that point in ministry in the prophetic movement, in the prayer movement and in church planting, but as I stepped ashore on Great Barrier Island that was all finished. As far as the condition of my heart was concerned, I was effectively an atheist.

I have seen more and more people leave ministry and reject Christianity because they cannot sustain what they think it takes to be a successful Christian. In truth, I have no problem with that kind of crisis because a Christianity that is not flowing from the experienced love of God is not real Christianity.

When I came to the Inheriting the Nations School the first thing that impacted me was not the stunning revelation that was being taught. I didn't even know that it was stunning revelation until I was willing to open my heart to it, for revelation and spiritual life always affect the heart that is open. When I met the team, however, it was a relief to discover how ordinary they were. They were down-to-earth men and women, without pretence but full of love. Then, when I heard James and Denise Jordan speak, I knew immediately that I could trust myself to them and open up my heart to what they were saying. They had been through everything that I had been through in life and more. I was able to identify with them in their Christian experience and their words had an impact and credibility that many others had not.

As I said before, I had sat in many meetings and listened to many speakers who I knew had not been through what I had been through so their words carried little authenticity for me. I opened my heart to James and Denise because they spoke from a place of burnout in ministry and a failed effort to serve God. Their words carried the depth of revelation that I was yearning for. Some statements made an immediate impact on me such as, "It's not enough to know that God loves you; you need to experience God loving you." Another statement was that, "love is a substance." The cry of my heart was to experience the substance of that love.

Within the first week I received the comfort that my soul so desperately needed. God the Father was able to pour His foundational comfort into my life. I was able to feed directly from *El Shaddai*, the "Many-Breasted One," - lying on my bed each afternoon I could feel pumping sensation pass through the top of my head and down through my entire body. That pumping sensation was the supernatural infilling of God's comforting love.

At the most basic level of humanity, our primordial need is for mothering comfort. The foundation of Christianity is the comfort of a parental God. Jesus lived and ministered from the bosom of the Father, and Paul the apostle did all that he did because of a foundation of comfort in his life (2 Corinthians 1:3-5). I had thought that the apostle Paul was a Christian superhero, far above anything anyone else could attain to. I now believe that he knew how to continually access the comfort that was available to him in God.

The issue of being a religious person is not so much the need to be 'saved'; it is the need to be comforted. At the very core of a religious person's identity there is a vacuum of comfort. If a religious person receives comfort, they will be religious no more. That is why Jesus said to Nicodemus the Pharisee that he must be born again. Nicodemus rightly understood that Jesus was talking about re-entering the womb; however, it wasn't the womb of the natural mother that he needed to re-enter. He needed to be reborn from the womb of God and grow afresh in an environment of deep and original comfort. When Paul spent those years in the desert after his Damascus Road encounter, he wasn't so much getting his theology re-configured; he was being comforted. When we are comforted by God, our theology will automatically be reconfigured. I was like Paul, I had been a "Pharisee of the Pharisees," and now I was being deeply comforted in the desert place.

A shocking realisation began to dawn on me. Throughout the entirety of my Christian life I had been living in an 'Old Covenant Christianity.' I had been living in a sophisticated matrix of religion which had its origin in my own self. Even my 'charismatic' experience of moving in the gifts of the Spirit and occurrences of the tangible presence of the Divine had done nothing to affect the deep-seated core of self-generated effort within me. It stunned me to realise that I was actually still only, spiritually speaking, a little baby. James Jordan puts it like this, "If you are a beginner in love, you are a beginner in Christianity because God is love." A statement like that puts the issue very starkly. I knew that I was addicted to eating from the Tree of the Knowledge of Good and Evil, and had never discovered what it was to eat of the Tree of Life. On this little island in the Pacific Ocean, I was beginning to feed from the Tree of Life.

We are beginning to see that what flows out of the revelation of the Father is a completely different type of Christianity to what we have known before. It is the real thing. In saying that, let me emphasise that this is not a new type of Christianity or a new diversion from the orthodoxy of the faith. Rather, it is a return to that ancient faith that the apostles knew. It is an ancient faith because it is coming from the Source Himself.

When we don't have a Christianity that flows out of the Father's heart, our faith is not built on the right foundation. A Christianity that only relates to Jesus and the Holy Spirit will still be infected with religion because God the Father remains an unknown quantity. The reality of the Gospel is that the Father sent the Son so that we would be brought back home to our deepest place of belonging and find our place abiding where Jesus abides, in the bosom of the Father.

Why I am Writing this Book

This book is motivated from my own experience. I write from a perspective of having burned out in the radical pursuit of the kingdom of God. I failed spectacularly as an 'on-fire' servant of God. I became completely exhausted with hard-driving, performance-oriented "Christianity." What is more, I *continue* to fail and I *continue* to be exhausted with that form of Christianity. However, I have discovered something else, and that is what this book is about: I have discovered what it means to be loved by God.

This book has its basis in the revelation of the love of the Father as specifically taught through the ministry of James and Denise Jordan. It is intended to be read within the context of the whole perspective of what they teach.

I have identified a number of areas in which we can discern whether we are relating to God in a religious way or not. There are some questions to be answered and some observations we can make which help us to identify whether we are still on the futile quest of religion. These five areas can be stated as follows:

1. *Where is the source of true spiritual life? What is the origin of Christianity?*

2. *In what direction does the movement from the source go? In other words, where is the destination and focus?*

3. *What is the central revelation of Christianity?*

4. *Christianity and religion need a mediator to bridge the gap between the human and the divine. But where does the mediator come from? Who does the mediator represent? What is the task of the mediator?*

5. *What about Sacrifice? How does sacrifice work in religion, and how does it work in true Christianity?*

By looking at these five areas, I will show what religion is and what Christianity really is. My goal is to expose the religious motivation that we are all vulnerable to. By doing this, I am confident that we can be set free from the exhaustion of religious pursuit, and learn to relax in the confidence that God is the initiator and energiser of true Christianity.

This book is written as a prophetic perspective. As such, it is not my intention to present a balanced view or to take into account other aspects of our life in God. This book is intended to open our eyes to see *how* we are relating to God. I hope that it will be prophetic enough to undermine the influence of religion, and to set the heart free to embrace what it means to be a beloved child of God. The prophetic pulls down and uproots but it also builds and plants. I believe this book does both.

CHAPTER ONE

The Difference Between Religion and Christianity

~

*"If your Christianity is not working for you, there is only one conclusion you can make. What you are experiencing **is not Christianity.**"*

— James and Denise Jordan

Many Christians believe that they are happily free from religion. They compare their lives to those of previous generations and believe that they are free from religious rules. But going to the movies on a Sunday or having the freedom to drink alcohol is no guarantee of freedom from religion. Religion is a much deeper human problem and freedom from it involves a much more radical solution than joining a trendy church or even giving up going to church.

Oftentimes we can receive a touch of the Father's love, and our emotions begin to be healed. We can attend a conference and feel wonderful. Then, when we return to our normal lives, somehow the feelings wear off and we lose our confidence in the love of God and His interest in our lives. This is largely because we are still infected by the virus of religion.

My definition of religion is this: it is where the initiative in relationship with God comes from us rather than from Him. Religion is where you and I are making the effort to know God and to please Him without any prior revelation of His love and His acceptance of us.

In true Christianity, everything comes from the Father. He is the source of our life, and everything flows downward and outward from His heart. That is the Christianity that Jesus lived and that the apostles had a stunning revelation of. Jesus did not rely on His own self-motivation. There was a love behind the love of Jesus. It was a primordial love, a source-love, and He lived out of that love. It was the love of His Father, whom He addressed as "Abba."

Both religion and Christianity operate in the same arena; in the gap between God and humanity. Whatever religion you choose, whether it is a monotheistic religion, a polytheistic religion, a world religion or a little known primitive religion, it operates in this gap. All religions *and* Christianity seek to connect God and humanity together.

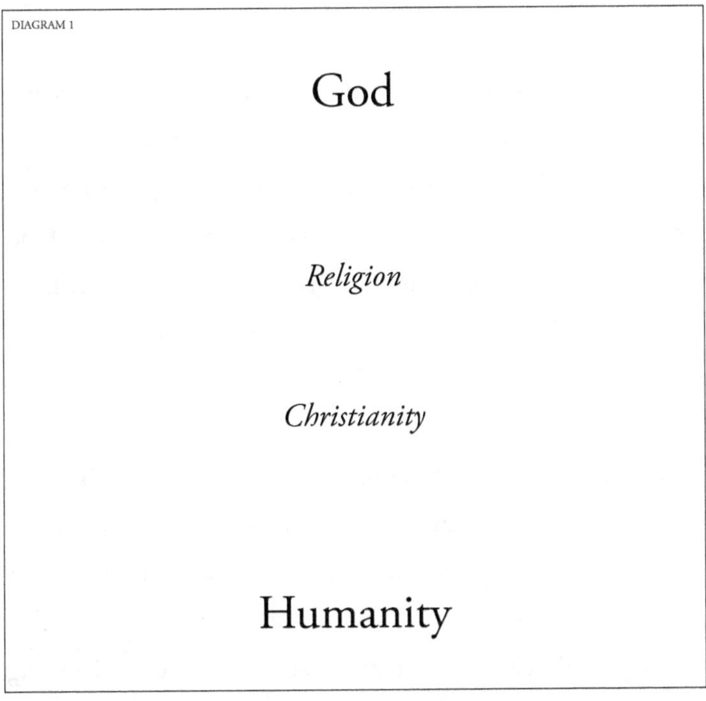

So...what is the difference? What makes real Christianity different from religion? The answer to this question took me forty-five years to discover. It is shocking in its simplicity, yet deeply profound in its implications.

The main difference is that religion and Christianity move

in different directions. One goes from the bottom up, the other goes from the top down.

Do you know which is which?

Religion is an upward movement in one direction. It starts at the human level and reaches upwards, attempting to reach God. This is the movement that I was on for most of my life. Christianity is a downward movement which begins in God and flows downward to humanity. Christianity comes from the heart of the Father and it flows in one direction, from Him to us. (SEE DIAGRAM 2)

If we can grasp this paradigm, it will bring everything into perspective. Many things in the Bible which may seem to be confusing, now become clear. It also makes sense of the things that happen in our lives. The truth is, living life out of this paradigm will make Christianity actually work for us. Reading this little book alone will not do that, but the substance and reality that it talks about will.

As I have stated already, both religion and Christianity operate in the same arena, the space between God and humanity. The crucial difference is the direction in which they move. Where does the initiative come from? What is the goal to which they are moving?

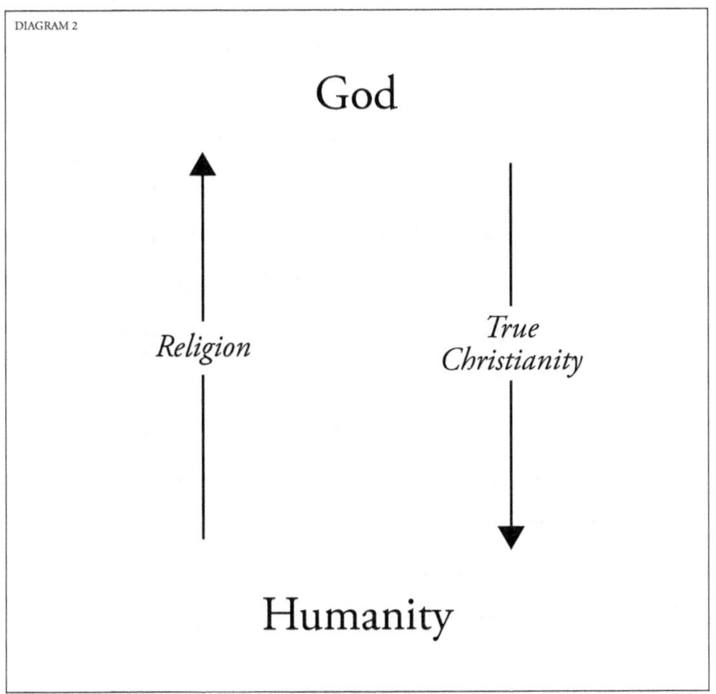

The Religious Quest

Let me explore this further. In Acts 17:16-27, the apostle Paul was in the city of Athens.

Now while Paul was waiting for them at Athens,
his spirit was provoked within him as he saw that
the city was full of idols. So he reasoned in the

synagogue with the Jews and the devout persons, and in the marketplace every day with those who happened to be there. Some of the Epicurean and Stoic philosophers also conversed with him. And some said, "What does this babbler wish to say?" Others said, "He seems to be a preacher of foreign divinities"—because he was preaching Jesus and the resurrection. And they took him and brought him to the Areopagus, saying, "May we know what this new teaching is that you are presenting? For you bring some strange things to our ears. We wish to know therefore what these things mean." Now all the Athenians and the foreigners who lived there would spend their time in nothing except telling or hearing something new.

- ACTS 17:16-21

Paul then addresses the Greek philosophers:

So Paul, standing in the midst of the Areopagus, said: "Men of Athens, I perceive that in every way you are very religious. For as I passed along and observed the objects of your worship, I found also an altar with this inscription,

'To the unknown god.' What therefore you worship as unknown, this I proclaim to you. The God who made the world and everything in it, being Lord of heaven and earth, does not live in temples made by man, nor is he served by human hands, as though he needed anything, since he himself gives to all mankind life and breath and everything. And he made from one man every nation of mankind to live on all the face of the earth, having determined allotted periods and the boundaries of their dwelling place, that they should seek God, and perhaps feel their way toward him and find him. Yet he is actually not far from each one of us..."

- ACTS 17:22-27

Paul perceived that they were very religious. Why? Why was it so readily apparent to Paul that these men were very religious? They were religious because they were caught in the upward movement of seeking an unknown God. They were trapped in the futile, up-stretching quest to perceive God through their own searching, but their eyes were closed to the God who was already near. When God is revealed we discover that, "He is actually not far from each one of us." He is revealed to be the One who pursues after us. When we find God, we discover that it is not we who have been seeking after Him, but it is He who has been inexorably seeking us.

Paul then goes on to set out what the religious quest looks like:

In verse 27 he says:

> *...that they should seek God, in the hope that they might feel their way towards Him and find Him.*

This expresses, in a nutshell, the futility of the religious quest. We do not need to find Him by our efforts or striving because He has already revealed Himself. What we do need is for the eyes of our hearts to be opened to see that revelation. When the eyes of our hearts are opened, God becomes real and immediate to us.

Christianity is not a quest to find a distant and obscure God. Christianity begins when our eyes are opened to see the God who is already there. In Ephesians 1:17, Paul asks that the Father may give us a "spirit of wisdom and revelation" to know Him. Christianity begins with the revelation of who God really is and flows from there.

The religious construct is founded on humanity hoping to feel its way towards God and find Him. Paul, however, then states what the reality is. The reality is that God is "...*actually not far from each one of us.*" (v.27). The reality is that, from the beginning, God has initiated a way to find humanity. According to Paul, at the level of creation, *all* humanity is God's offspring, and all humans (at the basic level of life in the created order) find their being in Him, for "in Him we live and move and have our being."

God was once the object of my Christianity but I discovered that I was the object of *His* Christianity. My Christianity began in my initiative, but when I burned out, I could not live Christianity in my energy any more. To my surprise I discovered that Christianity was actually not my life. Christianity was the life of God, and I was to be the recipient and container of the life that God lives. Christianity is not generated in my effort, my zeal or my willpower. The generative power of authentic Christianity is in the life of God Himself. Real Christianity is the life and love of the Trinity directed outwards towards us and then to all creation.

CHAPTER TWO

Where does Christianity Originate?

~

"All this is from God, who through Christ reconciled us to Himself..."

- 2 CORINTHIANS 5:18

"He is the source of your life in Christ Jesus..."

- 1 CORINTHIANS 1:30

The first point of difference between religion and true Christianity is revealed when we ask the question: Where is the source? Where is the life-source from which our connection with God is generated?

In religion, we are the source, and the initiators. Religion is initiated by humanity in order to attain to Godlikeness and its destination is God.

In total contrast, the source of Christianity is to be found in the heart of God, in His life and in His heavenly reality. Christianity is initiated by a God of love. What is more, real Christianity is the life that God Himself lives. Too often, we see Christianity as a lifestyle of choices based upon a particular set of beliefs or a life lived as a response to what God has done for us. The problem here is that we still live in the energy of our own life within us. We live a 'Christian' life out of the power of our own mind, will and emotions.

God is not to be the object of our Christianity. Rather, He is the subject of Christianity. We are the object of *His* Christianity. Real and authentic Christianity, as God intended it to be, is what Jesus lived, what Paul and the early Christians lived. True Christianity is a movement that originates in and gushes from the heart of the Father. Christianity flows from heaven to earth and ultimately, according to Romans 8:19 - 22, to the whole created order.

God did not become a Christian when Christ died on the cross. God was always "a Christian." The Trinity has always been living the Christian life. The basic issue is not so much about 'Christianity' as a theology or belief-system; it is about the life of God. What the New Testament writers are talking about is the metaphysical reality of the life-energy of God the Father, Son and Holy Spirit, the life that sustains Them in Their eternal existence. That life is the source and the fountain of our existence too.

The label of 'Christianity' has been so misused and corrupted that it is tempting to abandon it altogether. However, it may be better to redeem the understanding of what it really means to be Christian. The label 'Christian' was originally a disparaging one, attached to those in "the Way" (Acts 11:26). It meant 'little Christs' or 'Christ-ones.' What was meant to be an insult is actually more accurate than many of the perceptions of the word 'Christian' today. Christians are very much intended to be little versions of Christ Himself!

As I stated earlier, God has always been living the Christian life. God did not get more revelation when the Holy Spirit came at Pentecost. The death of Jesus on the cross didn't set God any more free than He already was. The whole point of Jesus' death on the cross was to bring *us* into the life that the Trinity *already* lives. Love is the substance of who God is. The truth is that we are the recipients of the life that God lives and of the love of His heart. This is the Christianity that Paul lived. He lived downstream from the Source, on the receiving end of eternal life.

Before he met the ascended Christ on the Damascus road, the apostle Paul was trapped in the religious paradigm. Paul's relationship with God was perpetuated entirely by his own willpower. He relates this in Philippians 3:4-6:

> *"...though I myself have reason for confidence in the flesh also. If anyone else thinks he has reason for confidence in the flesh, I have more: circumcised on the eighth day, of the people of Israel, of the tribe of Benjamin, a Hebrew of Hebrews; as to the law, a Pharisee; as to zeal, a persecutor of the church; as to righteousness under the law, blameless."*
>
> - Philippians 3:4-6

Religion is nothing less than "confidence in the flesh." It is our reliance on our own ability to find God and to enter into relationship with Him. Religion does not actually require any reliance upon God Himself. When Paul writes later in Philippians of "straining forward...for the prize of the upward call of God in Christ Jesus," he is *not* on the upward trajectory of religion. Paul's "upward call" was to live in the heavenly dimension of resurrection life. The call heavenwards is a call to be a receiver of the river of love that proceeds from God's throne.

Paul, as Saul of Tarsus, was confronted by the risen Christ on the Damascus Road. Falling literally and spiritually off his high horse, he was blinded by the glory that came out of heaven. He found himself, as it were, on the other side of my diagram; that is, on the side of receiving the downward movement of love. His eyes were re-opened to see true Christianity which originated in God. The foundation of Paul's life became a foundation of comfort. He lived in and operated out of the comfort that he continually received from the "God of all comfort." (2 Corinthians 1:3-5).

FOUNDATIONAL REVELATIONS
ABOUT GOD AS SOURCE

When I say that God is the source of true Christianity, what exactly do I mean? To answer this, I need to go to the first principle of all reality. In philosophy, a 'first principle' is a basic, foundational proposition or assumption that cannot be deduced from any other proposition or assumption. It is the absolute original reality that all other truth proceeds from. In Christianity, when we go to the source and allow revelation to flow from there, we will discover something more superlative than we have ever known before. We will discover original and authentic Christianity as God experiences it.

The entire canon of the Bible opens with these words:

"In the beginning, God..." - GENESIS 1:1

When we read this statement, it is crucial to know who this "God" is and what He is like. "In the beginning, God..." is not, of itself, a Christian truth. Neither is it a Jewish truth. Every religion can say, "in the beginning, God..." What makes Christianity unique is that it provides the answers to who this God is, what He is like, what motivates Him, what His specific purposes are, and how He achieves them.

Some texts within the New Testament contain revelation about the purpose of God in eternity, outside of the created time-space dimension. It is precisely here that we *must* look to find our starting point. These statements in Scripture allow us to glimpse into the root of existence. This is as far back as we can possibly see. It is not possible to go any deeper or any further back than the pre-existing purpose of God. We cannot go any farther back than the heart intention of the eternal Trinity.

GOD'S DNA

Another way to deepen our realisation of God as Source is to understand what He is made of. This may seem a slightly strange line of enquiry but consider this: If we were to take a DNA sample from God and test it under a microscope, what would it consist of? What is God's DNA? Of what substance is He formed?

There are only three statements in the Bible that describe the DNA or central essence of God's nature. These are not attributes but descriptions of spiritual matter. These three statements are all short and simple, and they tell us what God's substance is:

> *God is spirit* - JOHN 4:24

> *God is light* - 1 JOHN 1:5

> *God is love* - 1 JOHN 4:8

These are three nouns that describe the substance of God. God has many attributes but these nouns describe the *essence* of who He is.

Scripture states, for example, that God is "holy" but that is an adjective, a descriptive term used to describe a noun. The Bible doesn't say that, "God is holiness." Similarly, Scripture describes God as merciful, but it doesn't say that "God *is* mercy." All of God's attributes such as mercy, wisdom, holiness flow out of and are contingent upon His essence of spirit, light and love.

It is not sufficient to say either that God is a lover. Undoubtedly, He is a lover but the Bible goes further than that, to the ultimate statement that God *is* love. Holiness, mercy, judgement, justice, wisdom do not describe the *essence* of God. Rather, they flow out of His essence which is pure love.

God *is* love. He is not just a lover; He is Love itself! Everything in the Scriptures that God says or does must be understood in the light of the fact that He is love. This is helpful to know when people try to balance the love of God as an equal attribute to His judgement, or say that He is equally Judge to being Father. He is not! The judgement of God is a reality but it is *always* the judgement of One who is Love itself.

THE TRINITARIAN COMMUNION

The Source of Christianity is located within the loving circle of the Trinity. John's statement "God is Love" (1 John 4:8) is a Trinitarian statement. It points to a communion of love. If God is love, God is one, but God must also be a community. There is one God, but a tri-unity of Persons. Love must have a subject and an object. When we read "God is love," we see inter-personality within the essence of the Godhead, before any creation, whether of angels or of humanity.

When we explore the nature of the Trinity we must always remember that it is clothed in mystery. The Father is God; Jesus is God; the Holy Spirit is God. All three are of the same substance; all are, in their essence, God. However, they have different functions within the communion of the Godhead. Before Jesus came to earth, He was the Son of the Father. He was in the Father's bosom, embraced by the Father. In some way that we do not fully comprehend, He was drawing from the Father as Source. In some way that is veiled in mystery, the Father was fathering Jesus eternally. Jesus was not created, but He was, in the words of the Nicene Creed, "eternally begotten of the Father." The Father is eternal Source; the Son eternal Manifestation. The Holy Spirit is the love between the Father and the Son, a love so substantial that it is a Person[1].

Because God is love, that love is always seeking to express itself to its object. There is no death in heaven but there is complete self-giving from divine person to the other. Love

---

1. C S Lewis, following Augustine of Hippo, puts it like this, "What grows out of the joint life of the Father and Son is a real Person, is in fact the Third of the three Persons who are God (*Beyond Personality*, New York: Macmillan Co., 1948, pp. 21f.)

always wishes to give of itself. It cannot stay self-contained but always goes out to the beloved. The disposition of the Father was always to give Himself completely in love to His Son. Love loves to love, and love *must* love. It cannot do otherwise.

The cross is an eternal disposition in the heart of God. The Son never desired anything that was contrary to the desire of the Father. He was always willing to go to the place of being pleasing to the Father and satisfying the Father's desires. He always had a son's heart towards His Father. The Lamb was slain from the world's foundation (Revelation 13:8). From eternity the cross was also an attitude of the Father's heart. He was willing to give His Son, and in his Son to enter the human race to bring forth a bride for the Son. Paul tells us that, "God was in Christ reconciling the world to Himself" (2 Corinthians 5:19). The Son was willing to lay down His life to bring many sons to glory (Hebrews 2:10).

Jesus' prayer to His Father in John 17 lifts the veil on the loving relationship between the Father and the Son. Verse 5 of John 17 elucidates this:

> *"And now Father, glorify me in your presence*
> *with the glory that I had with you before the*
> *world existed."*

> *- JOHN 17:5*

This glory was the glory of divinity and of having the same essence. It was *also* the glory of the Father-Son relationship.

The apostle Paul also brings forth revelation of God's essential parenthood in Ephesians:

> *"For this reason I bow my knees before the Father, from whom every family in heaven and on earth is named..."*
>
> - EPHESIANS 3:14

This verse can be also read, "from whom *all fatherhood* in heaven and on earth is named." All true fatherhood draws its nature and character from the Father. From the very beginning God is Father. He is essentially 'parent.' The Source of everything is in the parenthood of God who is love.

WHAT DOES GOD REALLY WANT?

Another question which must be considered when we read Genesis 1:1, is what does this God, who created "in the beginning," actually want? What does He desire? What are His purposes? What is on His heart? If we didn't have New Testament revelation, we would have no way of answering these questions. The New Testament outlines how the redemption story hangs together, beginning and ending with God, whose substance is light and love. Love, therefore, is the substance of the author and inspiration of the Scriptures. We need to look at the Bible through a revelatory lens of the truth that Jesus brought about the Father. Without the love of God we have a distorted image of everything.

Let me look at some texts which again give us a glimpse behind the time-space veil into the redemptive purpose of God:

"...that they may all be one, just as you, Father, are in me, and I in you, that they also may be in us, that the world may believe that you have sent me."

- JOHN 17:21

Jesus is affirming the Father's purpose that we might be in Him and in the Son. The Father wants us to live in Him; that we would know what it is to be caught up into His life, and for His love to be resident within us.

The wonderful thing about failing to be an effective Christian is the realisation that *His* life is the only life-force that is really operating. In retrospect, it is a wonderful thing to 'hit the wall' and burn out because we then discover the wonderful principle that is at the heart of true Christianity, the principle of death and resurrection. The Father is not intimidated by death, failure, or crisis. He knows that out of death comes resurrection. On this basis, a faith crisis becomes an opportunity for hope and anticipation. If our faith is coming to an end, what an opportunity! Why? Because the faith of the Godhead is much more powerful than our faith. When we come to the end of our energy, something else can happen: the life of the Trinity can begin to flow.

There is only one person in the universe living the Christian life—God Himself. Jesus, when He was here on earth, didn't even live the Christian life from His own resources. He lived in absolute reliance upon His Father. The Christian life is an energy that comes from heaven. It is the life of God, which He lives in and through us. The sooner we can realise that there is a great stream of life coming from the heart of God the Father that has been issuing from eternity, then *real* Christianity begins.

The New Testament writers clearly understood this perspective. Paul, in particular, spells out the eternal genesis of the Christian life. The following passage from Ephesians throws light upon this reality. So often we read texts like this from a 'Jesus only' perspective, but this passage is full of the Father's intent and action. I have identified in brackets who Paul is referring to in this passage, showing the role of the Father and the role of the Son.

> *"Blessed be the God and Father of our Lord Jesus Christ, who has blessed us with every spiritual blessing in the heavenly places in Christ; even as He (the Father) chose us in him (the Son) before the world's foundation, that we should be holy and blameless before Him (the Father) in love. He (the Father) marked us out beforehand for sonship through Jesus Christ to Himself, according to the good pleasure of his (the Father's) will, to the praise of the glory of His (the Father's) grace, with which he (the Father) has taken us into favour **in the Beloved**. In him (the Son) we have redemption through his blood, the forgiveness of offences, according to the riches of his (the Father's) grace, which he (the Father) lavished upon us, in all wisdom and insight making known to us the mystery of his (the Father's) will, according to his (the Father's) purpose, which he (the Father) set forth in Christ as a plan for the fullness of time, to unite all things in him (the Son), things in heaven and things on earth.*

*In him (the Son) we have obtained an inheritance,
having been marked out beforehand according to
the purpose of him (the Father) who works all
things according to the counsel of His (the Father's)
own will, so that we who were the first to hope in
Christ might be to the praise of his (the Father's)
glory. In him (the Son) you also, when you heard
the word of truth, the gospel of your salvation, and
believed in him (the Son), were sealed with the
promised Holy Spirit, who is the guarantee of our
inheritance until we acquire possession of it, to the
praise of his (the Father's) glory."*

- EPHESIANS 1:3-14

The Father's purpose is not so much to bless us because He loves us. His purpose is to bless us "in the Beloved." We are caught up and carried into the sonship of Christ.

Colossians brings out the same perspective:

*"May you be strengthened with all power,
according to his glorious might, for all endurance
and patience with joy, giving thanks to the Father,
who has qualified you to share in the inheritance
of the saints in light. He has delivered us from*

the domain of darkness and transferred us into the kingdom of the Son of his love, in whom we have redemption, the forgiveness of sins."

- Colossians 1:11-14

The Father Himself has qualified us to share in this inheritance. The source of everything and the power to sustain it comes from the Father. We do not qualify ourselves. Even if I go through a crisis of faith, I know increasingly the power of death and resurrection, and I am growing ever more confident in His qualifying of me. Our entrance into the kingdom of the Son of His love, is by becoming loved *in the Son*. Until we gain confidence in the revelation of His love, we have a residual tendency to think that the Father is reluctant about including us in His plans and purposes. Nothing could be further from the truth. The truth is, *we* are the focus of the Father's purpose and His whole being is geared towards the fulfilment of His plan.

The kingdom of the Son of the Father's love is the true dominion. Only the one who is the son of a Father's love who can exercise the dominion of the Father's love. Any rule outside of love is not the kingdom of God, it is the domination of power. The rule of the kingdom of God is in the power of vulnerability in love. For many years I sought the power of the kingdom. I sought to wield spiritual authority and to gain anointing for a dynamic ministry of power. I didn't realise that love itself carries ultimate authority. Love brings power that cannot be resisted.

GLORY BEFORE THE AGES

But we impart a secret and hidden wisdom of God, which God decreed before the ages for our glory. None of the rulers of this age understood this, for if they had, they would not have crucified the Lord of glory. But, as it is written, "What no eye has seen, nor ear heard, nor the heart of man imagined, what God has prepared for those who love him"— these things God has revealed to us through the Spirit. For the Spirit searches everything, even the depths of God. For who knows a person's thoughts except the spirit of that person, which is in him? So also no one comprehends the thoughts of God except the Spirit of God. Now we have received not the spirit of the world, but the Spirit who is from God, that we might understand the things freely given us by God. And we impart this in words not taught by human wisdom but taught by the Spirit, interpreting spiritual truths to those who are spiritual.

- 1 CORINTHIANS 2:7-13

These verses communicate that God's "secret and hidden wisdom" in eternity was to give incomprehensible gifts to His sons and daughters, gifts which can only be revealed by the Spirit. The lavishness of the Father toward us is beyond human sense and imagination.

Do you realise that God has decreed our glory before the ages? The divine manifesto pronounces that humanity is to be glorified with the glory that God bestows. When we see Christianity from this perspective, it revolutionises the way that we live. *We human beings* are the object of Christianity, a Christianity originating in heaven, in the bosom of the Father, and culminating in the Father pitching His tent among us and within us. The movement works so that the Father would be manifested in our human life.

The apostle, Peter, also knew by revelation what was God's intent. According to 2 Peter:

> *His divine power has granted to us all things*
> *that pertain to life and godliness, through the*
> *knowledge of him who called us to his own glory*
> *and excellence, by which he has granted to us his*
> *precious and very great promises, so that through*
> *them you may become partakers of the divine*

*nature, having escaped from the corruption that
is in the world because of sinful desire.*

- 2 PETER 1:3,4

The more that our hearts are open to receiving from Him and the more that we grow in love, these two realities can co-exist within us. The Father indwells human nature, and humanity simultaneously partakes of the divine nature. This is only able to be experienced in love. The Father is glorified in our weakness; the treasure is contained in an earthen vessel. The whole point of the Incarnation is that the glory of divinity would be housed in a human tabernacle.

I used to think that the source of Christianity was in me; it was about me seeking and loving God. I now realise that God is not the object of my Christianity. I am the object of His Christianity. I am the object of His life and the object of the love of His heart. I sought God and loved God for many years and I became increasingly exhausted. In my religious pursuit, I didn't realise that I was wading upstream against the power of the current. When I collapsed in utter failure as a Christian, I began to sink beneath the water. I feared that I was drowning. Then I heard the roar of the Niagara Falls of the love of the Father. Its waters buoyed me up and carried me downstream, past all of the landmarks I had traversed in my quest for the fountainhead. All along God had been seeking me and the Father had been loving me. The love of the Father is not a bolt-on or add-on to the Christian life. It is the foundation that *everything else* is built on. Everything else in Christianity flows out of the Father's love. Where is the source of true Christianity? It is in the Father's love.

Religion reaches up, Christianity flows down

~

*"Religion is, 'How do I get to God?' - Christianity
is, 'How do I let God get to me?'"*

- BRIAN ALLEN

"Everything is gift"

- JAMES JORDAN

As we have seen, the source of Christianity is God Himself and the source of religion is in humanity. However, the construct of religion has a deeper source than the human race. Religion has its roots in the heart of Satan himself. This is why it is so pervasive in culture and in the world system. The origins of religion can be traced to the very same source as the origins of orphan-ness. Orphan-ness entered the atmosphere when Lucifer rejected God as Father and was cast out of the presence of the Father's love. Religion is one of the main manifestations of being without the Father. It has its beginnings in Lucifer's desire to become like God. We see this in the prophetic insight given by Isaiah:

> *"You said in your heart,*
> *'I will ascend to heaven;*
> *above the stars of God*
> *...I will ascend above the heights of the clouds;*
> *I will make myself like the Most High.'"*
>
> — ISAIAH 14:13,14

What a noble ambition! To ascend into heaven to become like the Most High! (SEE DIAGRAM 3)

The upward movement of the religious quest began in Lucifer's ambition to make himself like God. We see this ambition illustrated also in the building of the Tower of Babel (Genesis 11), when the people of earth conspired to build a city and a tower reaching towards heaven.

It sounds very plausible. Many believers, including myself, have cherished this very desire - to be like God. Yet that is the major deception of religion, that we can make ourselves like

God. Lucifer didn't want to escape *from* God. He wanted to be *like* God, through his own self-generated effort. Lucifer's corrupted wisdom is the prototype of religion. Religion is a self-generated and a self-perpetuated quest which cannot possibly succeed.

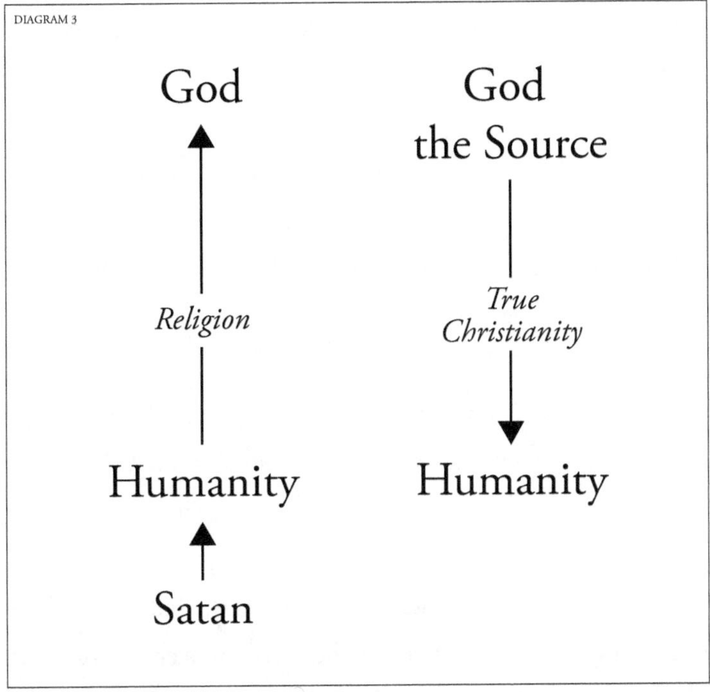

Many of us have tried to become like God through an upward move of self-determined effort. I progressed to the ultimate in this quest in my own life until I hit a wall in 2007 and fell down, only to discover that the river of life was actually flowing in the opposite direction. Grace always flows downwards to the lowest place, to our deepest depths. The movement of God is downward to meet us at our lowest place. In my low place, a permanent state of weakness and dependency on God, I find myself in the downstream of the "Niagara Falls" of love which flows from the heart of the Father. I am still at the bottom. Having fallen off the religious ladder, I now know that the lower I go, the more love and grace I can receive.

THE DOWNWARD MOVEMENT OF LOVE

The downward movement of God is vividly seen in the action of Jesus the Son:

> *"...who, though He was in the form of God, did not count equality with God, but emptied Himself..."*
>
> - PHILIPPIANS 2:6

The downward movement of the Son is the reflection of the heart and movement of the Father. This movement of Jesus (described in Philippians 2:6) has been named by theologians as "the Kenotic Movement." It comes from the Greek verb *kenóō* which means "to empty oneself." This kenosis is actually an attribute of the Godhead, the continual self-emptying of Itself in mutual love for Each Other. Love always pours itself out but it is continually replenished by its own intrinsic wellspring. The movement of Love is always an outward movement from itself; yet that outward movement constantly reaps its own reward.

EVERYTHING IS GIFT

In the New Testament, the divine strategy originates in heaven and comes down from heaven to earth. Everything from God comes to us as gift on the downward movement of love. The Gospel of John gives many examples of this flow from the Father through the Son to the people that His heart loved. He loved the children that He lost and sent the Son down so that He, the Father, could identify with the plight of orphaned humanity.

Enter into restful contemplation as you read these verses about the initiatives of the Godhead.

> *"...And the Word became flesh and dwelt among us."*
>
> - JOHN 1:14

The literal meaning of the word "dwelt" is "to tabernacle," or to "pitch a tent." Incarnation is the pitching of the divine tent among us and within us.

*"For the bread of God is He who comes down
from heaven and gives life to the world."*

- JOHN 6:33

*"This is the bread that comes down from heaven,
so that one may eat of it and not die. I am living
bread that came down from heaven."*

- JOHN 6:50

Jesus, as the "divine bread" came down from heaven. The food which gives eternal life is given from God.

"As the living Father sent Me..."

- JOHN 6:57

When the Holy Spirit came on the Day of Pentecost He descended from heaven to indwell us in our human weakness. Everything from God comes as gift on the downward trajectory - it is never earned through reaching up or striving. I love the phrase that James Jordan often uses, "Everything is gift." Brennan Manning expressed it another way: "All is grace." We cannot receive grace-gift by reaching upwards to achieve.

GOVERNMENT IN A DOWNWARD DIRECTION

One of the last images the Bible gives us in John's apocalyptic vision is the Holy City, the New Jerusalem descending out of heaven from God. The book of Revelation contrasts the government which comes down from heaven with the government which arises from earth. The kingdom of heaven is a descending rule of love. In absolute contrast, the government which comes out of the wisdom from beneath is an antichrist government. The New Jerusalem *descends* from its place of origin, whereas Great Babylon is built upwards. This Jerusalem is the Bride, descending from God, having originated in His life and in the womb of Heaven. The City is the vehicle of Love's administration. It is the expression of the government of love. Love always governs in a downward direction.

The Church does not have her origin on the earth. The Church has her origin in heavenly reality. She descends. The Bride is going to emerge out of the revelation of sonship. Individual sons and daughters will corporately become the Bride that descends out of heaven. It must be this way. The Bride, the New Jerusalem, can never emerge out of an orphan identity. The Bride must emerge and be given to the Son by the Father. As the revelation and experience of sonship is increasingly established within individuals throughout the earth, one day we will see the Bride emerging, coming down from the Source.

The angel invited John to see the Bride but what John actually saw was not a woman in a wedding dress; he saw a city coming down from heaven. When the Church comes to a place of governing and administrating in love, she will have come to the place of dominion (the rule of love) intended for the man and woman in Eden. The feminine Church, in harmony with the Head, Jesus Christ, will move in dominion over all creation. This will only become possible when Christ and the Church fully complement each other. When heaven and earth are aligned, healing and dominion come to creation.

A SPIRITUALITY OF IMPERFECTION

The eyes of the knowledge of good and evil are always looking for improvement and betterment. I once heard a preacher recounting a dream that he had the night before he was due to speak at a conference. In the dream, he saw two great serpents holding up the edifice of the religious system. God revealed to him that these were the twin demonic pillars of religion which were highly influential in the Body of Christ. The names of the two pillars were "Excellence" and "Responsibility." Striving towards "excellence" and taking "responsibility" to become more effective spiritually may sound plausible and good but they are (in the words of James 3:15) the wisdom that is "earthly, unspiritual, demonic." In contrast, the wisdom which comes from above and goes to the lower place is, "pure, then peaceable, gentle, open to reason, full of mercy and good fruits, impartial and sincere." (James 3:17).

Love truly sees its object for what it is. This is true wisdom. When we operate in the love of God, we are automatically flowing in the wisdom that comes from above. Love will always lead in the way of this wisdom, not necessarily in what is seen to be right and proper. Jesus offended the Pharisees because he broke the conventions of the law-code but Love always led him in the way of wisdom. Paul says (in 1 Corinthians 1:24), "...but to those who are called, both Jews and Greeks, Christ... the wisdom of God," and "...Christ Jesus, whom God made our wisdom..." (1 Corinthians 1:30). The love that we receive from the Father, forms Christ, who is the wisdom of God, within us.

In love, we cannot go wrong. When we are sons we do not so much need to seek guidance or "a word from the Lord." The place of sonship is actually freedom in love. Even if we make a mistake, everything is redemptive. Love covers every-thing (1 Peter 4:8) and can redeem everything. The perfect will of God is to be in the love of God. Then you will discover that "everything is permissible" (1 Corinthians 10:23). Love makes everything permissible but decides what is beneficial in a situation. The perfect will of God is to receive the Father's love and be transformed by it. The only requirement to mature from spiritual babyhood to sonship is to keep receiving the love of the Father. Paradoxically, spiritual maturity means more, not less, dependence.

The desire to be like God was the very thing that Satan tempted the woman with in the garden of Eden. Genesis 3:4-5 describes the serpent's trap, "You will not surely die. For God knows that when you eat of it your eyes will be opened, and *you will be like God.*" It is not wrong to want to be like God. Nevertheless, conformity to God's likeness happens in the downward movement. In order to become like God, we must switch direction from achieving to receiving. We become like God, not through determination or striving, but through receiving and abiding in His love.

The dazzling glory of Christianity is that God wants to come and indwell 'little old me.' I am finally beginning to believe in my heart that God is within me. A revelation of ourselves as God's dwelling place is as important as a revelation of the Father Himself. Why? Because the love of the Father is found, not by looking upwards but by looking inwards, into our hearts. The human heart is the portal for the perception of heavenly reality. We need a revelation of the extent of the Incarnation. When we begin to realise that Christ is within us, we possess the hope of glory. The great revelation that is coming to the Church now is who we are in God. In God, we are sons caught up in the sonship of Christ. The next revelation, to go hand in hand with this one, is who God is *in us*. This is the mystery that was hidden (Colossians 1:27), that Christ in us is the hope of glory.

I am no longer trying to escape from my brokenness. It is in my flimsy tent that He delights to dwell. The resting place of God is in my humanity as it is *right now*. I do not need to improve my tent, for He will transform it by His resting presence. I long for the day when the revelation of this sweeps through everyone. If we expect progress on the side of the upward movement, the communities that grow out of the love of the Father indwelling broken humanity can often disappoint us. Weakness and ordinariness are very disappointing to the religious progressive. In sonship, we are not making much progress towards excellence, but we are making progress to the lower reaches of grace. We find that much revelation flows here, in the sacrament of a few ordinary people who are learning to love each other without any fig leaves. This revelation of the Father's love will not bring us to more 'excellence'. It will lead, however, to more weakness, more freedom, and more glory. It will see Him released and manifested through our weakness.

CONDESCENDING GENTLENESS

Love descends in gentleness to make the beloved great. It is only love that can change anyone to be like God. The Darby Translation renders Psalm 18 like this:

> *"And thou didst give me the shield of thy salvation, and thy right hand held me up; and Thy condescending gentleness hath made me great."*
>
> *- PSALM 18:35*

That verse holds the secret to becoming like God. David realised that to become like God was to receive the condescending gentleness of the God who stoops down. There was no point in making an attempt to ascend to heaven. Heaven has always been coming to earth.

God, in His condescending gentleness, comes down into our broken humanity and transforms it as His ability seeps into our inability. He then raises us up with Christ to sit with Him in heavenly places (Ephesians 2:6). Any upward movement is a movement of resurrection out of death by the glory of the Father. As for Jesus, same for us. In fact, we have died and been buried with Him, and are raised again with Him and seated in heavenly places. All this is done by God. The Father doesn't stay locked up in heaven, as a great monolith without any emotion. God is not inscrutable. The Father Himself is filled with self-giving love which constantly stoops down.

I have learned a lot through being a dad of two little children. One of the most physically challenging aspects of fatherhood for me is having to stoop down all the time, to get down on the floor and then back up again. Every time I need to change the baby's dirty nappy, I have to get down onto the floor. The whole point of fatherhood and motherhood is to constantly stoop down to the level of the little ones, to attend to them, to lift them up, to put on socks and shoes that have come off, to clean them up, to engage and play with them.

Our heavenly Father is like this. Before I became a father, I was used to living on a higher level, the level of adulthood, but parental love always stoops down. God the Father is a downward Mover; Love Itself meets us where we are. My children are being made 'great' by my condescending gentleness to them. They are being made 'great' by the constant attention of their mum, stooping down to their level. As they receive love they grow up naturally to our level. They do not grow by self-effort but by receiving the condescension in love of their parents.

In many churches nowadays there is a "culture of excellence." A "culture of excellence" is on this upward movement. It is little more than religion in a subtle guise. People cannot ever sustain enough 'excellence' to match what an 'excellent' God is supposed to expect. The truth is, God is not 'excellent' based on our value-system, nor is He impressed by our excellence. God, the Trinity, is meek and humble, and willingly accepts our imperfection.

The concept of a perfect God, in the way that we understand it, is actually not a biblical concept. Rabbi Abraham Joshua Heschel, speaking from a Hebraic paradigm, has made this statement:

> *"The notion of God as a perfect Being is not of biblical origin. It is not the product of prophetic religion, but of Greek philosophy; a postulate of reason rather than a direct, compelling, initial answer of man to His reality. In the Decalogue, God does not speak of His perfection, but of His*

having made free men out of slaves. Signifying a state of being without defect and lack, perfection is a term of praise which we may utter in pouring forth our emotion; yet, for man to utter it as a name for His essence would mean to evaluate and endorse Him. Biblical language is free of such pretension; it dared to call perfect (tamim) only "His work" (Deut. 32:4), "His way" (II Sam. 22:31), and the Torah (Ps. 19:7). We have never been told: "Hear, O Israel, God is perfect." [2]

The love of God is actually *tolerant* of imperfection. Striving after 'excellence' in the spiritual life precludes freedom. The love of the Father ultimately produces the freedom that He Himself enjoys.

We tend to overestimate our maturity in the spiritual life. If we saw ourselves as spiritual babies, who have not progressed to spiritual solids yet, we would be so much easier on ourselves. We would not be under so much pressure to perform and please God.

Young children do not have the remotest interest in a culture of excellence. Rather, they enjoy a life of freedom

---

2. A. Heschel, *The Prophets*, New York, 1962.

and self-expression. The onus is on the parents to develop the family culture. The more we become like little children we will find that the culture of our Father's house flows down into our lives. The culture of the Father's house falls like rain, sometimes in a torrential downpour, sometimes in a light drizzle, with all the varying intensities between. It is a culture of nurture, love, and freedom.

Good parents have grace for the messiness of a burgeoning life. How much more does God, the perfect parent, have grace for the messiness of the burgeoning life of the heart? I long for the day when the Body of Christ gets rid of a quest for excellence, and we all become free in our expression of who Jesus is within us. The love of the Father is going to release us to be our true selves and true reflections of His personality.

One of the major keys of how I came to experience the Father's love for me, was that I felt relaxed within a community where individuals were free to be themselves. I believe there is a "sacrament of ordinariness" in which glory streams from broken vessels. I was able to identify with James and Denise Jordan because they too were at the bottom of the downward movement, receiving the Father's compassion and grace for their lives. Like me, they had spectacularly burned out and collapsed on the upward movement of serving God. Through identifying with them, I was given grace to transition to a place of receiving the Father's love pouring down over me. To my surprise, I found that His grace and His acceptance flowed to my lowest place. Just as water will always seek and find the lowest level, so the love of God always seeks and finds the lowest level of human existence.

Understanding what grace really means frees us from the need to become excellent. The Father's condescending gentleness to you will transform you into the image of the Son. As you abide with Jesus in the Father's bosom, you will become like Him.

The real issue of being a child of God is to continually receive from the Father. Mature sonship then reciprocates the love that it has received. The default position of a son is always to be downstream from the Father. It is to be constantly receiving from Source, to live a life from that Source, to allow the Source to reproduce Its life. Sonship lives from the fathering and mothering love of its Source, receiving nurture and comfort, strength and revelation.

It is only the love of God that can transform us to be like God. Nothing else can do this. All my life, I tried desperately to be like

God. After many years on the religious quest, I came to realise that only receiving His love could actually make me like God.

CHAPTER FOUR

Christianity is the Revelation of God as Father

~

"The Christian life is a return to the Father, the Source, the Ground of all existence, through the Son, the Splendour and Image of the Father, in the Holy Spirit, the Love of the Father and the Son."

- THOMAS MERTON

The next distinction between religion and true Christianity is that religion has an unknown, generic deity whereas Christianity is based upon a specific revelation of who God is. God, in His essential being, is Father.

This is not merely nitpicking at semantics. What we believe about God deeply affects the life that we live. It has far-reaching implications for the degree of peace that we experience and how much freedom we walk in. It deeply determines the level of rest and contentment that we have. A statement by James Jordan constantly challenges me: "You can tell how much of the Father's love you are experiencing, by the amount of fear and worry that you have in your life. If we really believed that our Papa was Almighty God, we wouldn't be able to worry if we tried!"

If our revelation of the God who is the source of everything does not extend beyond an Old Testament revelation of Yahweh, the life that we live in response to that belief will be the life of one who is under command, and not at rest. I still struggle with fears and worries but they are diminishing because the revelation of who He really is, is continually seeping through to my heart. The God of wonders, the God of the heavenly armies, the God of the ancient patriarchs, has been revealed in my heart to be "Papa." The many titles that He is known by in the Old Testament are all subsumed within the name of "Papa."

Religious Speculation about God

Paul, the apostle, summed up the quest of religion as seeking "the unknown God." In his speech at the Areopagus he nailed the definition of religion:

"Men of Athens, I perceive that in every way you are very religious. For as I passed along and observed the objects of your worship, I found also an altar with this inscription, 'To the Unknown God.' What therefore you worship as unknown this I proclaim to you..."

- Acts 17: 22,23

Religion, in its widest sense, has sought to define the God who is unknown. It has done so on the basis of speculation, projection and constructing a false personality of who God is and what He requires. This speculation and construction is done in the absence of revelation about who He really is.

Not knowing who God truly is as Father, means that there are no guarantees in this life or beyond. Therefore, we are forced to develop and maintain a religious system, a form of worship, to keep on the right side of the deity that we do not know. There is no absolute guarantee that God will favour us and bless us, so we need to do all that we possibly can to earn favour and blessing, and to avoid potential retribution. This 'God' may someday turn His back on us, let us down, abandon us and judge us. He may well withhold favour on the basis of our non-conformity to what He requires. We are not assured of His absolute goodness and love for us so we must generate and sustain this upward movement. The only option is to follow the upward pointing arrow. Our life will be a life which consists of building altars to "the Unknown God." (SEE DIAGRAM 4)

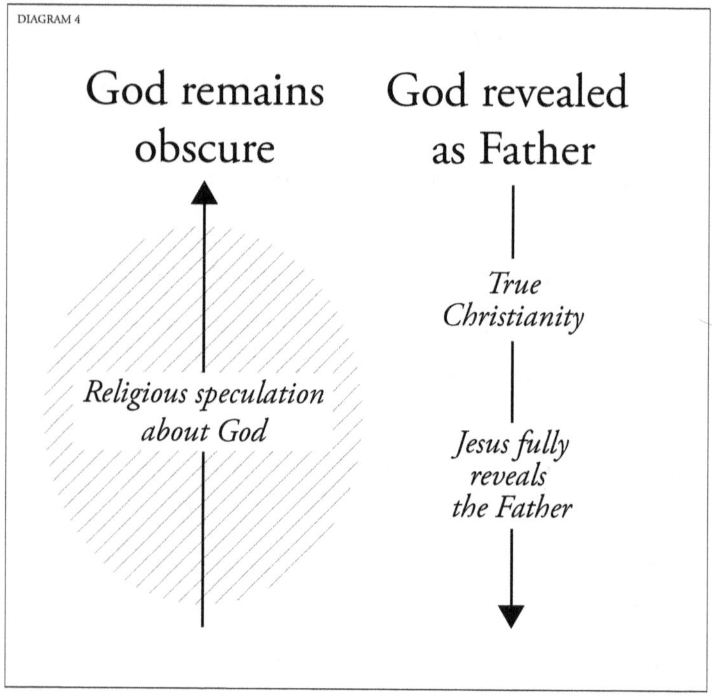

Even as a 'mature' Christian, my life consisted in building altars. I was a radical servant of King Jesus, but God the Father and Jesus as *Son* remained unknown. Because God had not been revealed to my heart as 'Abba', I saw Him through the eyes of orphan-ness, as One in whom there is no guarantee.

I couldn't rest in Him, or throw my life into His hands, trusting His unconditional love. I had a theology for God the Father but His fatherhood had not been revealed to my heart, nor His parenting made experiential in my life. I continually strained to discern the perfect will of God because, outside of His perfect will, there was no blessing. If I didn't hear the voice of God accurately and obey His command to the letter, I would be outside His blessing, and life would not go well for me. All of the initiative had to be on my part, all of the energy generated and maintained by me, because God would not shift His position. A God who is not a Father is immoveable and intransigent in the face of human weakness and suffering.

It was easy for Paul to perceive that these philosophers were extremely religious, for they had "objects of worship." These objects were most likely the Greek gods. Then, to cover the bases, they had an altar dedicated to "An Unknown God." Every religion, to one degree or another, has erected this altar to a God who is unknown. All religion is based on an incomplete revelation of the true nature of God. This is a continuum because some are closer to His true character than others. As an evangelical Christian, I had an obscure revelation of who God is; I had a mental assent to the doctrine of the Trinity but experientially, I only knew Jesus as Saviour and Lord. As a charismatic Christian, I knew about the Holy Spirit (to a limited degree) but I had no experiential knowledge of the Father. The One who sent Jesus and the Holy Spirit was vague and generic - only known to me as 'God.' Then, in 2008, I had a revelation specifically and experientially of God the Father. In His essential nature, He is Love, He is Source and, most definitively, He is the Father of the Lord Jesus Christ, and He is my Father. Through that revelation I now know where I stand with Him. I stand on an unshakeable foundation because I know what He is like.

CHRISTIANITY HAS MADE GOD KNOWN SPECIFICALLY AS FATHER

Christianity never really worked for me until I met the Father. Let me make a statement which some may find controversial. If we have a Christianity that has no connection with the Father, it must essentially be a religious Christianity. A Christianity minus sonship is a servant-hearted Christianity. It is orphan-spirited Christianity.

Paul's description of the Original and Supreme Being as, "...the God and Father of our Lord Jesus Christ" (Ephesians 1:3), is a fulsome and all-encompassing theological statement. It leaves no doubt as to God's nature and personality. The point of connection for us as human beings is the Lord Jesus Christ but the Source, and simultaneously the Destination, is the God and Father of the Lord Jesus Christ. A Christianity that is missing the revelation of the Father is still actually a religious Christianity. If we have not entered into the rest of the Father's arms, then we have not ceased from our own works (Hebrews 4:10). However, we cannot cease from our own works until we have a revelation of the Source in His specific nature - that of loving Father.

The starting point of an authentic Christianity for me was when I came to know Him as Father. It was the inception of a Christianity which began to change me from the inside out, transforming my personality as I learn to live in the ongoing experience of the Father's love for me. The Christianity that I had lived on the upward trajectory of religion didn't change my personality, make me a more loving person or give me any peace. Furthermore, it didn't make me any more morally righteous or more like Jesus.

1 John 1:5 tells us that "God is light and in Him there is no darkness at all." That is a very important statement. A lot of theology is based on darkness. I don't mean darkness in a sinister or occult way. When the Bible talks about darkness, it means a lack of revelation. Obviously, the occult and evil is based on a complete misrepresentation of who God is, but *all* religion is based on a lack of revelation about who God is.

Religion thrives when we begin to speculate about the truth of who God is. This is human conjecture through the eyes which perceive only right and wrong, good and evil. When the serpent put the question, "Did God say?" to the woman, he was effectively challenging her to speculate about the true nature of God. Since that time, there has been a temptation in the human mind to speculate in the gaps between revelation.

Let me explain further: We get a revelation about one particular truth. Then we get a revelation about another separate truth. We then employ our natural minds to speculate, to try to logically join the two revelations together. This is where we create a false theology. Human speculation can never replace divine revelation. If you have a question about something for which you have no revelation, resist the temptation to formulate an answer. Enter into rest, and ask the Holy Spirit to answer your question by revelation. We must trust the Holy Spirit to fill the gaps in revelation, by giving *fresh* revelation. If we do not do this, our human speculation begins to develop a theology that doesn't flow from revelation. True Christianity, and the only Christianity that really works, is the Christianity that flows from the revelation of the Father.

God did not become Father when Jesus came to earth. He always was Father, the Source and the Sustainer of all life.

The revelation of the Father that Jesus brought to earth, and the post-resurrection witness of the Spirit, declare what has always existed. The Son and the Spirit have both testified that the Father is the Sender and the Source:

"As the living Father sent me, and I live because of the Father."

- JOHN 6:57

"...yet for us there is one God, the Father, from whom are all things and for whom we exist, and one Lord, Jesus Christ, through whom are all things and through whom we exist."

- I CORINTHIANS 8:6

"...one God and Father of all, who is over all and through all and in all."

- EPHESIANS 4:6

That God the Father is the Source has also been the understanding of the Church throughout history.[3]

---

3. For any theologically minded readers who may be wondering about the Filioque controversy, this comment by the Catholic theologian, Stratford Caldecott, clarifies the current climate: "Naturally there are differences between Eastern and Western Christians here, since the East has traditionally rejected the idea that the Spirit proceeds from the Son as well as the Father - but these differences have now largely been overcome, for example by reference to the traditional Eastern formulation that the Spirit proceeds from the Father *through the Son.*" S. Caldecott, *The Radiance of Being: Dimensions of Cosmic Christianity,* Tacoma 2013.

THE COUNCIL OF NICAEA (A.D. 325):
"We believe... in our one Lord Jesus Christ the Son of God, the only-begotten born of the Father, that is, of the substance of the Father, God of God, light of light, true God of true God, begotten, not made..."

THE COUNCIL OF CONSTANTINOPLE (A.D. 381):
"We believe... in one Lord Jesus Christ, the only-begotten Son of God, born of the Father before all ages, light of light, true God of true God, begotten, not made, consubstantial with the Father"

THE ATHANASIAN CREED (A.D. 400):
"The Father is not made nor created nor begotten by anyone. The Son is from the Father alone, not made or created, but begotten... Let him who wishes to be saved, think thus concerning the Trinity. But it is necessary for eternal salvation that he faithfully believe also in the incarnation... He is God begotten of the substance of the Father before time, and he is man born of the substance of his mother in time."

PATRICK OF IRELAND (A.D. 452):

"Jesus Christ, whom we... confess to have always been with the Father—before the world's beginning, spiritually and ineffably [he was] begotten of the Father before all beginning"

- CONFESSION OF ST. PATRICK

Here are two contemporary theologians:

KALLISTOS WARE [4]

"The first person of the Trinity, God the Father, is the 'fountain' of the Godhead, the source, cause or principle of origin for the other two persons."

STRATFORD CALDECOTT [5]

"Thus the Father is the source of Son and Spirit, the Son is begotten by the Father and also has a part in sending the Spirit, and the Spirit is 'breathed forth' by the Father and Son."

This prophetic revelation of the love of the Father has been spearheaded in our time by Jack Winter, and James

---

4. K Ware, *The Orthodox Way*, St. Vladimir's Seminary Press, Crestwood, New York, 1995.
5. S Caldecott, *The Radiance of Being: Dimensions of Cosmic Christianity*, Angelico Press, Tacoma, 2013.

and Denise Jordan, among others, to bring what has been accepted as doctrine into experiential reality. The revelation of the Father will become the paradigm through which all truth is known and it will affect everything, not least of which will be how we read the Bible. The principal interpretive key to the Scriptures is through the nature of God's substance which is love.

JESUS REVEALED THE FATHER

Christianity is about the revelation of Jesus but that is not all. Christianity is about who Jesus came to reveal. Christianity is the revelation of the Father. I truly believe that everything outside of the Father's love is nothing more than religion. It doesn't matter how trendy or culturally relevant the Gospel presentation is; if it suggests reaching upwards to impress God or to be more like Him by anything other than the in-breaking of His love, it is a religious system. If there is no experiential revelation of Father, there will be uncertainty about God's true nature, and therefore, there *must* be a religious system. Alternatively, we could call this 'Old Covenant Christianity.' The Gospel of John bears this out:

> *"And the Word became flesh and dwelt among us,*
> *and we have seen His glory, glory as of the only*

Son from the Father, full of grace and truth. (John bore witness about Him, and cried out, "This was He of whom I said, 'He who comes after me ranks before me, because He was before me.')

And from His fulness we have all received, grace upon grace. For the law was given through Moses, grace and truth came through Jesus Christ. No one has ever seen God; the only Son, who is in the bosom of the Father, He has declared Him."

- JOHN 1:14-18

This passage sets out the contrast between the two covenants, the Old and the New. It contrasts Moses, the mediator of the Old Covenant, with Jesus the Mediator of the New Covenant. Moses did not have a revelation of the Father; therefore, all that he could bring was a code of law. The One who came from the bosom of the Father brought an abundance of grace and truth. Another way to talk about 'grace' and 'truth' is to use the terms 'gift' and 'reality'. The only reality of knowing the Father is that *everything is gift*. Christianity demands nothing from you apart from a willingness to receive the Gift. The true nature of God can only be declared by the Son who abides continually in the bosom of the Father. This is the place from where the Gospel is declared; the Gospel is declared *from* the bosom of the Father. It is manifested from an environment of nurture and comfort. The Good News comes from the merciful heart of the Father.

Christianity is the revelation of God specifically as Father, through His Son and in the power of the Spirit. Christianity is Sonship! The Jews knew who Yahweh was, and they knew His attributes. Those who were not Jewish, the Gentiles (or 'the nations') did not have this knowledge. But those who were near and those who were afar off have, through Jesus, "access in one Spirit to the Father." (Ephesians 2:17,18) Access in one Spirit to the Father brings those who were afar off into close proximity, and those who were outsiders into the family. Jesus came to reveal to us the life that he was living, and to bring us into his life with the Father. The end goal of the Gospel is that we would be united with him in the life that he is living with the Father and everything that flows from that.

God's cosmic purpose is to redeem us to His family. This is why heart forgiveness of parents is the linchpin to entering into a relationship with the Father. Above everything else, forgiving from the heart is about redeeming the relationship with our parents. God is, more than anything, our eternal Parent. We can dull the edge of this issue of heart forgiveness to extend to other authority figures who may have hurt us, but that is a subsidiary point. Forgiveness of others may be important, but it will not redeem a parental relationship. The core issue of redemption is the redemption of the parental relationship. If a child is secure in the love of its parents, the unkind words or actions of other authority figures will roll like water off a duck's back. The eternal place of destiny is the Father's bosom; from that deep belonging, which only the childlike can know.

God remains unseen and unknown until the Son comes forth from the bosom of the Father, and declares who He really is.

In religion, the promise of union with God is continually dangled at arm's length. It will never, ever happen. It is like a mirage in the desert, always on the horizon but never reached. In Christianity, however, the promise of union with God is actually made real in our hearts and in our spirits. The promise of being united with Christ happens immediately and can be experienced in the now, in every minute of every day. Religion always holds out two caveats which separate us from God - time and distance. In other words, God is distant right now but maybe, one day, we will be close to Him. When the light of revelation comes and the Father's love pours in, the time that is coming (John 4:23) becomes now and here.

Jesus Christ proclaims that we can know the Father in the immediate. Receiving the substance of the Father's love removes the barriers of time and distance.

TRUE WORSHIP

Jesus brought forth this reality in His dialogue with the woman at the well of Sychar. We read this in the narrative of John 4:

> *The woman said to him, "Sir, I perceive that you are a prophet. Our fathers worshipped on this mountain, but you say that, in Jerusalem is the place where people ought to worship." Jesus said to her, "Woman, believe me, the hour is coming when neither on this mountain nor in Jerusalem will you worship the Father. You worship what you do not know, we worship what we know, for salvation is from the Jews. But the hour is coming and is now here, when the true worshippers will worship the Father in spirit and in truth, for the Father is seeking such people to worship Him."*
>
> - JOHN 4:19 -24

In this passage, Jesus clearly stated that the revelation of Christianity is specifically about knowing the Father. This woman initially recognised Jesus as a Jewish rabbi. She didn't know who He really was, but her revelation progressed as the dialogue at the well went on. It went from 'sir' to 'a prophet' to 'the Messiah'.

Originally, this Samaritan woman had a generic understanding of God. The Samaritans worshipped Yahweh, as the Jews did, but they were despised by the Jews. They worshipped in a different location and according to a different code than the Jews. The major issue between Jews and Samaritans was the location of the chosen place to worship God. For the Jews it was the temple in Jerusalem, while for the Samaritans it was Mount Gerazim. Her dialogue with this man at the well began for the woman with the age-old question: where was the right place to worship God? Jesus appeared to side with the Jewish tradition when He said, "...we worship what we know, for salvation is from the Jews." But then He cut across centuries of theological debate to make a prophetic statement:

> *"But the hour is coming and is now here, when*
> *the true worshippers will worship the Father in*
> *spirit and the truth."*

The true prophetic will always cut cleanly and sharply through theological speculation and sectarian debate, to bring a deeper and more primordial reality.

> *Jesus declared, "Woman, believe me, the hour is coming when neither on this mountain, nor in Jerusalem, will you worship the Father. You worship what you do not know, we worship what we know, for salvation is of the Jews."*

Jesus was speaking to her from the perspective that she believed him to be, a Jewish rabbi. He said, "We worship what we know, for salvation is of the Jews." The Jews had their doctrine and system of worship correct according to the rubrics of the tradition. Jerusalem was indeed the proper location to worship God. But Jesus said, "The hour is coming," - but not only is it coming, it is now here. Jesus collapsed the time delay between the future and present, and forcibly pulled the future into the present. The hour is coming - and now is. When the Father is revealed, the time now is. When the love of the Father is experienced as substance in our hearts, it carries with it the fulfilment of all that prophecy hopes for.

This woman did not have a revelation of the Father. She said, "We worship *God.*" The knowledge of who God is was still not personal to her and, as a result, her worship was reduced to a formula. She, like the Jews, was fixated on an external system in a particular geographical location. It was a matter of 'this mountain' or Jerusalem. The priority was outward form. For religion, outward form determines inward reality. For true Christianity, however, inward reality invades and permeates outward forms. In other words, if the heart is right, we can choose any outward form, and it will be worship in spirit and in truth. If I am a true son, I can worship spontaneously or with a liturgy, and it will still be in spirit and in truth. The form of worship is not the point; the heart of worship is.

The Father is seeking such to worship Him. A generic revelation of God, without having the specific revelation that he is Abba Father, invariably leads to a systematised form of worship, a worship that is located in soul rather than spirit, and which has a diminished reality rather than the full reality. It may be a sophisticated form or an inferior form, 'Jerusalem' or 'this mountain,' depending on your viewpoint, but it is still a system. Knowing the Father liberates us from system and formula into life flowing from the innermost being and the true self.

I lived most of my Christian life caught in divisions as to the correct way to worship. The Body of Christ today cannot come to agreement as to what is the best mode of worship. Some may believe that worship coming out of the latest songwriters is a superior form to Gregorian chant or vice versa. This is all missing the point, however. Jesus brings out the reality that, without the revelation of the Father, all varieties of worship will in some way miss the mark.

Worship in response to the revealed Father is a worship that goes beyond the soulish realm and is from the innermost depths of the spirit. Our whole life becomes worship from the deepest, innermost core of our being. We respond from the reality that can only be seen in the light of the Father's love.

CHAPTER FIVE

Where does the Mediator come from?

~

"He who is from God; he has seen the Father."

- John 6:46

"Since then we have a great high priest... Jesus, the Son of God."

- Hebrews 4:14

Another difference between religion and Christianity is identified by looking at where the mediator comes from. This is very important. The one who reconciles between God and humanity, who bridges the gap - where does this go-between come from? Where does the Mediator originate and where does the Mediator go to? By answering this we will be able to understand something very profound and yet very simple.

This will reveal the vocation and mission of the One who mediates between God and man. The vocation and mission of Jesus, as Mediator, is to reveal the Father, and to bring many sons (male and female) to the glory of familial reunion with the Father.

Let's go back to our original diagram. Both religion and Christianity operate in this same space. A mediator is clearly needed to bridge the gap between God and humanity. (SEE DIAGRAM 5)

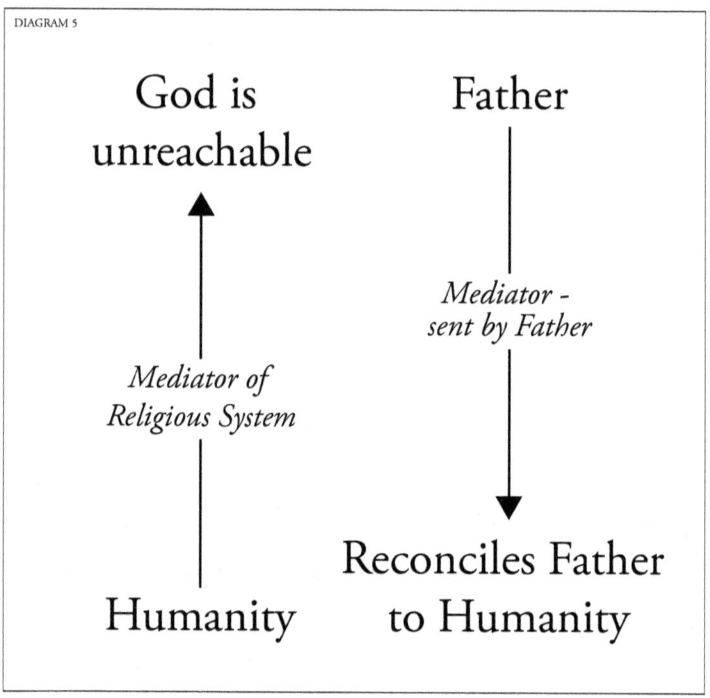

THE ORIGIN OF THE MEDIATOR

In religion, the mediator is chosen by men to represent them. The mediator is one who comes from mankind to bring them into the presence of God. The religious mediator is appointed on the basis of merit; that is, they are somehow considered to be more worthy to approach God. They have become more 'pure,' more 'holy', more 'competent' and therefore more qualified to stand as a representative of a people trapped in self-disqualification. The majority of people feel ashamed, and see themselves as naked and unworthy of connecting with God. Consequently, a system is created whereby a select group, who are perceived to have qualified, go to God on behalf of the others.

In authentic Christianity, the go-between has a different origin. The mediator comes *from* God. The Mediator is chosen by God to act on behalf of God. It was the Father who sent the Mediator, His Son, Jesus Christ. What does that tell us? It tells us that God the Father took the initiative to reach fallen humanity. He wants to relate to us infinitely more than we want to relate to Him. This gives us an abundance of hope and confidence. Be assured of this reality: that He is for us. The mediatorial role of the Son was initiated by the One who sent Him, His Father.

Jesus annunciates very explicitly in John's Gospel the sending action of the Father. I invite you to meditate on these portions of the sacred text:

> *"...and we have seen His glory, glory as of the only Son from the Father."*
>
> - JOHN 1:14

The words "from the Father" show that Jesus perfectly expressed all who the Father is. For almost two millennia, Christianity has been disconnected from who the Father is because of our own lens in relation to fatherhood, but also because of a lack of revelation. Since the early days of the Church, the revelation of the Father has been missing. Generally speaking, the Church has not connected that Jesus is the Son of the *Father*. The New Testament makes it very clear that the Mediator *came from* the Father.

> *"For God so loved the world that He gave His only Son, that whoever believes in Him should not perish but have eternal life. For God did not send His Son into the world to condemn the world, but in order that the world might be saved through Him."*
>
> - JOHN 3:16, 17

"...but He who sent me is true, and I declare to the world what I have heard from Him."

- JOHN 8:26

"...this charge I have received from my Father."

- JOHN 10:18

"Jesus, knowing that the Father had given all things into his hands, and that he had come from God..."

- JOHN 13:3

"But when the fulness of time had come, God sent forth His Son..."

- GALATIANS 4:4

The purpose of Christianity is not so much to reveal that Jesus is God, but to reveal that God is Father. Jesus came to reveal that Yahweh was actually Abba. The God of the Old Testament is, in reality, Papa!

In our servant-hearted Christianity there has been a disconnect between Jesus and the Father. Jesus is seen as kind and loving, merciful and tender-hearted, but the Father is not. The general perception is that the Father is either judgmental and vindictive or passive and uninterested. Our deep orphan-ness conditions us to perceive the Father wrongly. When we come to the realisation that it was the Father who sent the mediator, Jesus, we see that the Father is no different in heart motivation than Jesus. This allows us to trust the Father as being full of love, passionately and eternally motivated to reach fallen humanity.

I had reached an impasse in Christianity, not able to move beyond a relationship with Jesus as Saviour and Lord. For me, Jesus was the source of Christianity, and God the Father remained veiled to my heart. God the Father was surrounded by a cloud of mystery. Everything was centred around Jesus, and the Holy Spirit's primary role was to help me know and serve Jesus better. However, my heart still remained orphaned as long as the Father remained unrevealed and unknown.

Emphasising the place of the Father does not diminish Jesus. The purpose of Christianity is not so much to follow Jesus as a disciple, as to be united with Him in His sonship. When we come to the realisation that we are in union with Christ, we find ourselves to be in union with His sonship to the Father. We are in the Beloved.

Our hearts find rest knowing at a deeper and deeper level

that our Christian life is not dependent on us. The only thing to do - the simplest and yet often the most difficult thing - is to open our heart to receive. This repositions us to be downstream from our source, the Father. He is the fountainhead of the stream. Sonship is perpetually located downstream from the fountainhead.

Christianity has become stuck at the Mediator. It has focused on the Mediator but missed the work of the Mediator.

The best mediators or priests on the religious side are those who have achieved the highest rank. They are the ones who progress farthest on the upward movement of religion, through knowledge, correct performance, and through being perceived as being more competent or morally superior.

In Christianity, however, the mediator came from the opposite direction. The Mediator came down from heaven, and was sent by the Father. If we know by revelation that Jesus, as mediator, was sent by the Father, it changes how we see God. I used to believe, that humanity and the Father were at loggerheads with one another. My view was that God the Father was so angry and offended at the human race that He could not abide being in relationship with us. I believed that Jesus was the benevolent, mature, and responsible peacemaker who stepped in between the warring parties. My heart-belief, although I wouldn't admit it aloud, was that God couldn't tolerate the human race. Then I got a revelation that the Father sent the Mediator. The Mediator came from the Father to reconcile us back to the Father. The Mediator was the Son, who came to declare the Father's desire and intention.

This revelation pointed me back to what the Father was truly like. No longer could I separate the Father from Jesus. The Father had not turned His back on the human race. By sending the Mediator, the Father had initiated reconciliation. The Father sent His Son so that, instead of being in Adam , we would be in Jesus. In other words, we would no longer be orphans but sons.

When we look beyond the Mediator to see where He originated from, it becomes very clear where He is taking us. He originated from the Father and His work is to take us back home to the Father.

The Christian revelation is not so much about Jesus as Saviour, but about God as Father. Jesus is the Way and the Door. We come through Him to the Father. The purpose of the Mediator's work is that we might come freely to the Father and live in the sonship of Jesus. The Father is not passive or reluctant to receive us. He is reaching out, through Jesus, with open arms.

CONFIDENCE TO COME TO FATHER

The book of Hebrews, which is not easy to read, is actually *all about* sonship. We have only begun to scratch the surface of what is actually contained in this book of the sacred Scriptures. The Spirit has recently begun to open Hebrews up to me. I feel like I am walking in a lush garden bursting with many exotic trees and laden with fruit ripe for the picking.

The overarching aim of the book of Hebrews is to give us confidence to come near to our Father. The whole book can be summed up in this line from chapter 4:

"Let us therefore come boldly to the throne of grace."

- HEBREWS 4:16

My observation is that the vast majority of Christian do not have a confident and "bold" relationship with God. If we really understood what the writer to the Hebrews is bringing out, we would not hesitate to come to God. I have become increasingly confident in my relationship with God. I now know that I can come before Him 'warts and all.' I can bring my dark side into the Holy of Holies; I can come before the Father with absolute honesty about my weaknesses and the temptations that I face because Jesus has faced the same temptations (Hebrews 4:15). I now feel as relaxed in Father's presence as I do with my most intimate human friend. I trust the Father as much I have learnt to trust Jesus.

Hebrews 1:1 declares that God once spoke through prophets. However, God could never be revealed fully through prophets so He now speaks to us "in Son." This is what the original language of verse 1 says. The mode of God's revelation is "sonship." This is because God must be revealed as "Father," for this is who He truly is. This takes the revelation of God the Father beyond the individual historical person of Jesus when He walked on this earth. God's speaking "in Son" means that He is also revealing Himself through sons and daughters.

The revelation that Jesus *brought* is the ultimate revelation. However, the revelation of Jesus alone is *not* the ultimate revelation. The ultimate revelation is about Jesus and His Father, and our relationship to God as sons and daughters. The mode and language of the revelation of God is the language of sonship. The language that a person speaks reveals where they come from. God wants to be known by way of sonship.

He is revealed "in Son" because, in His purest essence, He is Father. The revelation of a son carries with it the revelation of his genesis, his father.

What the writer to the Hebrews shows is that the high priest and mediator of the Old Covenant was only a shadow that pointed to the true High Priest and Mediator, Jesus. Furthermore, the Mediator and High Priest of the reality (Christianity), in contrast to the High Priest of the shadow (the Old Testament), is a Son!

Hebrews 3 says:

> *"Therefore holy brothers and sisters, you who share in the heavenly calling, consider Jesus, the apostle and high priest of our confession..."*
>
> - HEBREWS 3:1

The core meaning of apostle is "one who is sent." An apostle is always sent as an ambassador on behalf of a sending authority. If Jesus was an apostle, who sent Him? The Father sent Him. The commissioning of the Son came from His Father's heart and His apostolic mission was a mission given to Him by the Father.

Jesus was sent by the Father to become the doorway back to the Father so that all the Father's children could come back home to the Father. The Father of Jesus is our Father too!

Hebrews 2 says:

> *"For He that sanctifies and those who are sanctified all have one origin. That is why He is not ashamed to call them 'brethren'..."*
>
> - HEBREWS 2:11

In religion, the one who sanctifies does not originate in the Father. In true Christianity, however, the one who sanctifies has His origin in the Father. What is the upshot of this? The upshot of this is that *we do not have to sanctify ourselves*. To be sanctified (made holy) actually means to "become other than," or to be "set apart." Only someone else can sanctify us and make us other than what we are, and that person is the Father. Our religious motivation to become like God using our own energy means that we strive to achieve some trumped-up form of morality. True Christianity takes the whole issue of sanctification out of our hands and puts it back where it belongs, to Jesus.

Hebrews 5:1 makes clear that "...every priest chosen from among men is appointed to act *on behalf of men*." In contrast,

Jesus "did not exalt Himself to be made a high priest, but was *appointed* by the One who said to Him, '*You are my Son...*'" (Hebrews 5:5). Jesus came in the opposite direction from every other priest. He came *from* the Father.

According to Hebrews, Jesus is a priest *in the order of Melchizedek.* There is a lot of speculation about the meaning of this. Simply stated, it means that Jesus' priesthood is a type of priesthood that predates the Old Covenant Levitical priesthood. Religious (and Old Covenant) priesthood mediates us to God. Jesus comes in the opposite direction; Jesus is a priest who came from God to mediate the presence of God *to us.*

Hebrews 7:3 tells us that Melchizedek was "*...without father or mother or genealogy having neither beginning of days nor end of life, but resembling the Son of God he continues a priest for ever.*"

What does this mean? It means that the origin of Melchizedek could not be traced through an earthly family tree. His father, his mother and his bloodline came from a dimension that was beyond our space-time existence. Melchizedek and his priesthood came *from* God. Hebrews 7:3 describes Melchizedek as "resembling" the Son of God. The Mediator came out of the eternal, heavenly dimension. Jesus is not a priest, nor does He mediate, on the basis of a human family line; He does so "by the power of an indestructible life." (Hebrews 7:16). His generation is one that has its origin in the Father.

When Jesus came, He came to reveal the substance of eternal life which is the relationship of the Son to the Father. This is the reality of the life of the Godhead. The Trinitarian community is a community of mutual, self-giving love, of inter-dynamic self-giving.

What the writer of Hebrews shows is that Christianity is not a new sect, not the new kid on the covenantal block, not a recent blow-in. On the contrary, true Christianity *pre-existed* Judaism. The revelation contained in the New Testament is more ancient and more primordial than that of the Old Testament. The writer to the Hebrews links Jesus to something that pre-dated Moses and the Covenant at Sinai. Hebrews connects Jesus to Abraham and to Melchizedek. Abraham's relationship with God was not about Torah observance or law-keeping. Abraham's relationship with God was based on divine promise and lived out by faith.

> *"Christ has obtained a ministry that is much more*
> *excellent than the old as the covenant he mediates*
> *is better, since it is enacted on better promises."*
> — HEBREWS 8:6

"In speaking of a new covenant, he makes the first one obsolete."

- HEBREWS 8:13

"Therefore he is the mediator of a new covenant, so that those who are called may receive the promised eternal inheritance."

- HEBREWS 9:15

In reality, the New Covenant is eternal. What biblical writers refer to as a 'new covenant' is not really new; it is only new in comparison to what was already familiar. What was familiar to the Jews was something temporary, a shadow-revelation of who God really was. Judaism believes that the Covenant of Sinai is eternal; in truth, it was temporary.

God wasn't under the Old Covenant Law when it was introduced. God was living in the utter fulfilment of the Law that Love already lives in. In the New Covenant, the Old Covenant Law is completely fulfilled because love fulfils every requirement of the Law automatically.

The Trinity has *always* lived in a New Covenant reality. It is a life of grace, of gift-giving, of the capacity and ability of God, of God's pleasure and satisfaction. The New Covenant gives us access into what the Trinity is already living.

The New Covenant is a commitment of love, and of the interaction of giving and receiving. This heavenly reality of the Trinitarian life is what the New Covenant is designed to bring us into. The New Covenant is what reconnects us with the Trinitarian family and restores to us the inheritance of sons and daughters.

The Old Testament is a shadow of the reality revealed within the New Testament. However, it is important to recognise that the New Testament in itself is not the substance. The New Testament *describes* the reality, in the same way that the menu in a restaurant describes what we can eat. The menu is not the same as the meal itself.

This is precisely why Hebrews does not mention the Father much. The Father is not encountered within the written words. He is encountered in the heart. As we go on the "new and living way" (Hebrews 10:20), we will be led to the Father.

The whole point of Christianity is to restore us back to the life of God as it is already operating. God who is spirit, light and love, is living in this New Covenant reality in the union of love. Each of the persons of the Trinity give of themselves for the sake of the others, because love always outworks itself in the giving of the gift. Love cannot remain locked up within itself. Love always has to move out from itself towards the object of its love.

Jesus did not come to mediate on His own initiative. If our revelation is situated there, we will be stuck on the way. God will remain obscure and intimidating, a commander to be obeyed rather than the Father of a family. One thing is sure, however. Intimacy with Jesus will ultimately bring us to the place of coming home to the Father. Jesus will never fail to declare who the Father is and to bring sons and daughters home to meet His Father. Coming home to the Father is inevitable, and the work of the Son and the Spirit to facilitate this outcome is guaranteed to be successful. We can rest in the truth that Father is delighted with us, and longs to bring us into the freedom that He Himself lives in.

CHAPTER SIX

The Re-Orientation of Sacrifice

~

"He does away with the first...to establish the second."

- Hebrews 10:9

The last issue I wish to tackle in this book is to ask the question: What about sacrifices, offerings and gifts? Does true Christianity demand us to live sacrificial lives, and to bring offerings and gifts to God?

The whole issue of sacrifices and offerings is so prevalent in the Bible and in religious culture that it cannot be ignored or swept under the carpet. Many people who react negatively to fundamentalism do so by trying to avoid and duck problematic texts in the Scriptures. That cannot be done, however.

We cannot dodge biblical texts that are seemingly difficult and contrary to the revelation of the New Covenant and the loving nature of our God. Yet, we can be confident that the Holy Spirit will bring the correct interpretation of the entire Scriptures in His timing. The more we see through the eyes of the heart and through the paradigm of the love of the Father the more we will see how the Scriptures fit together. The sacred Scriptures cannot be understood apart from revelation. Most theology is in the realms of human speculation, not divine revelation. But there is a revelatory theology coming through the spirit of wisdom and knowledge which comes from God.

Let me now tackle head on this issue of sacrifices, offerings and gifts.[6] Many people receive an experience of the Father's love but then revert to the old way of doing things. They do not come into sonship but continue in the same orphan-hearted, servant mentality of Christianity. They are living in 'Old Covenant Christianity' where there is an almost invariable pressure to sacrifice everything on the altar in order to be acceptable to God. This is precisely what led me to burnout and moral failure.

As this revelation about the re-orientation of all sacrifice began to dawn on me, I felt the need to anchor it biblically so

---

6. These three terms are interchangeable for my purpose in this book.

I decided to look at *Strong's Concordance.* This concordance cites 388 references related to the word 'sacrifice'; only around 50 of those occur in the New Testament, and most of them are about the death of Jesus on the cross. Furthermore, there are 377 references to 'offerings,' yet only 14 of which are from the New Testament. This tells us something particularly significant: there has been a sea change in the whole concept of sacrifice and offering.

The abolition of God-directed sacrifice

According to Hebrews, the death of Jesus ended forever all sacrifice to appease God. All sacrifice in the upward direction, as sacrifice towards God, ended with the death of Jesus on the cross. He gathered into Himself every sacrifice that had ever been made for sin and offered it to God. God's acceptance could no longer be earned (or perceived to be earned) within a system of continual sacrifice. Here are a smattering of verses from Hebrews 10 that leave us in no doubt about this:

> *"For since the law has but a shadow of the good
> things to come instead of the true form of these
> realities, it can never by the same sacrifices that
> are continually offered every year, make perfect
> those who draw near. Otherwise, would they not*

have ceased to be offered...?"

- HEBREWS 10:1,2

"...when Christ came into the world, He said, 'Sacrifices and offerings you have not desired, but a body you have prepared for me.
In burnt offerings and sin offerings you have taken no pleasure."

- HEBREWS 10:5,6

"...He abolishes the first in order to establish the second."

- HEBREWS 10:9

"But when Christ had offered for all time a single sacrifice for sins, He sat down at the right hand of God... for by a single offering He has perfected for all time those who are being sanctified."

- HEBREWS 10:12

Then comes the *coup de grâce*:

"For by a single offering He has perfected for all time those who are being sanctified."

- HEBREWS 10:14

In order to fully enter the rest that God has promised in the New Covenant, this is a crucial issue to understand. The death of Jesus ended all sacrifice to attempt to please God.

People often receive an initial liberating touch of the Father's love and then find that they do not progress to the true freedom of sonship. This Old Covenant understanding of sacrifice is so deeply ingrained that they remain trapped by it. The upward-reaching sacrifices of appeasement still carry on and the life-flow coming from the Father is stifled. The clear pronouncement of the book of Hebrews that Jesus has concluded all sacrifice to satisfy God has not yet been understood by revelation.

How often have we heard statements like, "God has been so good to you, and He has given everything for you, now you must pay back that by living a sacrificial life"? At first glance, this sounds very plausible, but it contains a serious deception. If God loves me so much, I need to live a life that pays Him back the debt that I owe to Him. That is sacrifice on the upward movement of religion.

What we need to understand is that sacrifice still works in the New Covenant, *but it works in the opposite direction.* Sacrifice has changed direction from an upward offering *towards* God to a downward offering *from* God. In the New Covenant all sacrifice flows in a downward direction from God the Father.

In religion, the weaker must always sacrifice to the stronger. Those with less resources must pay tributes to those with more. This can lead to spiritual abuse, where those in authority "lord it over" those who are under their authority (Matthew 20:25, 1 Peter 5:3). Poor humanity must sacrifice to God and His representatives. In true Christianity, however, it is the other way round! In true Christianity, the stronger sacrifices for the weaker. The Father sacrificed His Son, and His life in the Son. The Son lived by the life of the Father within Him and that life was poured out on the cross. In fact, we could say that the Father's life was poured out on the cross. The cross was a sacrificial act of the Father as well as the Son. "God was in Christ reconciling the world to Himself." (2 Corinthians 5:19). The Father sacrificed His own dearly-beloved, the Child of His bosom. The Son gave up His life in sacrifice so that the life of heaven would be available on earth. The Father and the Son gave freely of the Spirit to human beings. This never happens in religion. The God of religion is inviolate and beyond suffering.

New Covenant sacrifice works on the downward movement. It originates in the Trinity itself. The Father, as Source of the

Trinitarian community, is also the Source of self-giving. The source of the sacrifice of love is in the heart of the Father, who gave His Son, His beloved, for our sake. The Son, whose source was the Father, lived a life of love on this earth, constantly incarnating this self-emptying love of the Father. The Son, who possessed everything, sacrificed for the sake of humanity. The cross was a faucet that opened up the heart of God into a broken cosmos.

Jesus, as absolute image of God, radically shifted and redefined sacrifice back to its true definition.

I see more evidence of sacrifice where love is than I have ever seen in legalism or in radical servant-hearted Christianity. Love always surpasses duty. Love will actually motivate you to sacrifice, but it is sacrifice in the opposite direction from the sacrifice of duty. It is love that motivates a weary mother to get out of bed in the middle of the night to soothe her crying child. There is undoubtedly sacrifice involved in this, but it is by the mother, not the child. The stronger pours out for the weaker.

The stronger, those with more resources (be it material, physical, emotional, etc.) sacrifice in a downward direction so that love can flow from its source towards others. The Father pours His love out to others through words and actions as moved by compassion and prompted by His Spirit.

Jesus died to open the floodgates of the Father's love. The Holy Spirit, the very personality of God, was poured out from above, down into the human condition. You could say that God has taken a great risk to give of His personality to the messiness of our broken humanity. But it is the risk of love. It is no more of a risk than a parent who loves their little baby. Does love ever take a risk? The answer is a paradox. Love always risks because there is no guarantee of repayment. Equally, Love never risks because love never seeks repayment.

In the New Covenant, the principle and action of sacrifice is totally motivated by love. Love will automatically make a sacrifice for the benefit and wellbeing of the beloved. Any parent knows this. I have a child who is 4 years old and a child who is 2 years old. I can tell you this quite confidently - they never, ever sacrifice for me or their mother! We sacrifice for them all the time because we love them. We sacrifice our comfort, our resources and our life to give them better lives than we have experienced. Love doesn't hesitate to sacrifice for the sake of the weaker and the more needy. We, as parents, are the more competent and the stronger and so we sacrifice to manifest love to our little ones. This is the heart of God our Father. This is what the Father has done and what He continues to do.

In order to enter rest, the issue of sacrifice must be settled. The book of Hebrews tackles the issue of sacrifice because it is the big hindrance to entering rest. All sacrifice on the upward movement has ended with the death of Jesus.

In stark contrast, in the religious paradigm, sacrifices, gifts, and offerings are initiated in the religious heart. I want to offer the view that Lucifer, as the original religious spirit, offered sacrifice to try and become like God. I base my view on some words of the prophet, Ezekiel.

Ezekiel 28: 11-19 is a prophecy given to the king of Tyre, but it has a deeper meaning. It tells us about the fall of Lucifer, who became the Accuser, Satan. In verse 16 of Ezekiel 28, we read:

> *"In the abundance of your trade you were filled*
> *with violence in your midst, and you sinned."*
>
> *- Ezekiel 28:16*

What does this statement mean? Scripture doesn't tell us precisely what the nature of Satan's trading was. His goal was to exchange his place in heaven for the place of God. To trade is to offer something we already possess in exchange for something that we wish to procure. In the context of this verse, the practice of trading is actually the essence of orphan thinking. It is orphan because it works on the diametrically opposite principle of the kingdom of God: the economy of the Father's house and of His kingdom is gift giving and receiving, not buying and selling. All gift begins with the Father. Satan's "abundance of trade" was a rebellion against the culture of the Father's house.

"You were filled with violence in your midst, and you sinned." It may well be that Satan's violence was the violence of offering some kind of sacrifice in order to gain likeness to God. All sacrifice involves an act of violence meted out to a victim in order to satisfy the demand of another. Satan may have been the initiator of a sacrifice to barter so that he could ascend upwards and become like God. Maybe he tried to trade the place that God had allotted him in the heavenly panoply to gain a higher place. This was in direct contravention of the principle of sacrifice of the Father's house, the downward outpouring of love from the Father Himself.

I operated in a relatively sophisticated level of sacrifice until I burned out and my sacrificial edifice collapsed in a heap of rubble. Then I realised that sacrifice *began with Him*. He had sacrificed and was continually sacrificing to reach me. That revelation shifted me to be a receiver from God rather than an achiever for God.

Sacrifice as a redemptive manifestation of the Father's love

All sacrifice, therefore, after the death of Jesus is sacrifice which manifests God redemptively in and to His creation. Sacrifice works as a mechanism to incarnate the life of heaven on earth. It all works in a downward motion.

All of the following references to sacrifice and offering are biblical examples of this redemptive manifestation of the Father's love.

A prophetic foresight of it is given in Amos 5:

> *"Even though you offer me your burnt offerings*
> *and grain offerings,*
> *I will not accept them;*
> *and the peace offerings of your fattened animals,*
> *I will not look upon them.*
> *...But let justice roll down like waters,*

and righteousness like an ever-flowing stream."
- Amos 5:22-24

These verses are often used to applaud the merits of justice, compared with an insincere liturgy of worship. The point that I wish to make, however, is that it shows the change in direction of sacrifice. God shows that He is not satisfied with offerings and sacrifices which originate in human endeavour. The Hebrew meaning of 'burnt offerings' is literally "up-to-me ascent offerings." The response to this is something that flows down like a stream from its higher Source, and rolls like waters to lower levels.

In the New Covenant the sacrifices, gifts and offerings have come from God first. Religious sacrifice exists to please God, to effectively reach the object of our veneration. In contrast, New Covenant sacrifice exists to please God by facilitating this love to reaching the object of His love, humanity. A time is coming, and is now here, when the Father will reach through humanity to a groaning creation.

The human person was created to be a receptacle of the love of God. That is enough in itself. But the infilling of love cannot remain without an overflow. The human receptacle then becomes a channel of the love of God. The human person, compelled by the love of God, embodies the sacrificial attitude of God's heart.

According to Hebrews 10:5, this was how Jesus lived: He knew that the Father did not wish to receive sacrifice and offering, but rather wished to manifest His sacrificial love through Jesus:

Consequently, when Christ came into the world, he said, "Sacrifices and offerings you have not desired, but a body you have prepared for me;"

- HEBREWS 10:5

Jesus switched the source of sacrifice around. No longer do human beings offer God their sacrifices; God now offers His life through the body of Jesus to the world. Beginning with Jesus, the body of the Son (and sons) is the altar through which the love of the Father is manifested to humanity. Hebrews continues in verse 9:

"He abolishes the first in order to establish the second."

- HEBREWS 10:9

What does He abolish? He abolishes the old form of sacrifices and offerings.

What does He establish? He establishes the new form of sacrifices and offerings, by expressing the Father's will and desire through a body which has been prepared. The Incarnation began when God wrapped Himself in human flesh so that He could fully demonstrate His love and compassion to the human race.

> *"For from Him and through Him and to Him are all things. To Him be glory for ever. Amen. I appeal to you therefore, brothers, by the mercies of God, to present your bodies as a living sacrifice, holy and acceptable to God, which is your spiritual worship."*
>
> - ROMANS 12.1

I have included the last verse of the previous chapter to keep the flow of continuity here, and to see that the presentation of our bodies as a living sacrifice is the result of a much larger reality. The word 'therefore' always points back to the previous context; in this case, all things are from Him, through Him and for Him. Chapter and verse divisions are not part of the original biblical narrative, so we often take statements in isolation and don't see them as part of the bigger picture. The books of the Bible need to be read, at least initially, in their entirety at one sitting. That is how they were originally received and they were mostly read aloud to a listening audience. If we remove the chapter division and read Romans 12 as flowing on from Romans 11, we will see this verse in its proper context.

"For from Him, through Him and for Him are all things." On the basis of this reality, that all things are coming from Him, we can present our bodies. This is already presupposing that God is the Original Source, knowing that we cannot give what we have not first received. The sacrificial initiative has come from God and the stream of love is flowing downwards from Him through us. This injunction to present our bodies as living sacrifices is part of a thread from earlier verses in Romans. For example, *"the love of God is poured out in your hearts by the Holy Spirit,"* (Romans 5:5), *"there is therefore now no condemnation to those who are in Christ Jesus"* (Romans 8:1), and *"the Spirit helps us in our weakness"* (Romans 8:26). These are the foundations of any sacrifice that we make. Because the love of God has been outpoured in our hearts, because we are free from condemnation, and because we are helped by the Spirit in our weakness, we can then present our bodies. It is the body filled with love which is presented in sacrifice. The love-saturated body is offered as an incarnated expression of the Spirit of Parental love.

Note that it is a living sacrifice, not a dead sacrifice. It is the ongoing sacrifice of the living body which manifests the life of

God to others. Sacrifice of the body, as it meant here in Romans 12, means that the body stays alive. This type of sacrifice never hits the wall or suffers burnout. It is sustained by the Spirit and by love, not by the effort of the flesh. I offer my body as a living sacrifice to manifest the overflow of the love of God in my heart. If my child's nose is running and it needs to be wiped, and I am sitting in a chair reading a book, I need to offer my body as a living sacrifice to get up from my chair, cross the room, and bend down to wipe the child's nose. Compelled by love and compassion, I break out of the comfort of my chair and activate my body to help my child. This is on a very small and everyday scale but it works in the same way. Any mother will identify with this. A mother continually offers her body as a living sacrifice, driven by the maternal love in her heart.

Every time I go to another person and hold them in a sacramental embrace, I offer my body as a living sacrifice. Every time I speak forth revelation in front of a group of people, I offer my body as a living sacrifice. Christian ministry is the offering of our human faculties, our bodies, our will, our mind and our emotions to manifest the love of the Father. This is what pleases God. He is delighted to see His personality channelled through vessels here on earth. What is very clear to me is this: love always sacrifices much more for real results than the endless fires of useless sacrifice on the barren altars of religion.

What is acceptable to God is the presentation of our bodies so that everything from Him will be channelled to others. This is the sacrifice of sonship, the offering of the body in life. The charism of martyrdom involves the offering of the body in death, but true martyrdom only serves to open the floodgates so that the life of God can be extended. New Covenant sacrifice works so that the love of the Father can be spread abundantly on this earth, and released to those in need. A cup of cold water given in His name (Matthew 10:42) is the most basic example of this.

Everything in the New Testament, without exception, relating to sacrifice is to do with the outpouring of a God-filled human life towards others, in order to express God's life. The Father is a spirit. He needs a body to incarnate Himself within. He did so in his son, Jesus Christ. Now that Jesus is in heaven, what has happened to the incarnation of Father God in creation? It happens through His sons and daughters, through the body of Christ here on earth.

Paul the apostle was a conduit of giving and receiving blessing through New Covenant sacrifice. Here's what he says in Philippians 2:17 (NIV):

"But even if I am being poured out like a drink

*offering on the sacrifice and service coming from
your faith, I am glad and rejoice with all of you."*

- PHILIPPIANS 2:17

Paul wasn't being poured out to appease God. Paul was being poured out in the ministry of love within and towards the Body of Christ. And the sacrifice of the Philippians came from their faith. In other words, their revelation of the love of God was the catalyst for their sacrifice.

In the New Covenant, the sacrifice and the drink offering is not to satisfy the deity because of wrongdoing or to gain a favour. It comes from our faith, out of the love and acceptance within us, and is poured out to our brothers and sisters. Paul's letters and the writings of the other New Testament authors, without exception, identify all sacrifice as being sacrifice that is outworked in the life of the community. All New Testament sacrifice is God-sourced and individual, community and creation focused.

*"Through him then let us continually offer up a
sacrifice of praise - the fruit of the lips - do not
neglect to do good and to share what you have,
for such sacrifices are pleasing to God."*

- HEBREWS 13:15,16

The fruit of the lips is an expression of what is in the heart. The sacrifice of praise flows out of a heart filled with the revelation of who God really is. Again, the sacrifice comes from the revelation.

Notice that this sacrifice which is pleasing to God, is to share what we already have. God is pleased because He gets to release His resources through you and me. New Covenant sacrifice comes out of what we already have been given. It is the overflow of the gift. In the Father's love, the substance that we possess is fathomless.

> *"Therefore be imitators of God, as beloved children. And walk in love, as Christ loved us and gave Himself up for us, a fragrant offering and sacrifice to God."*
>
> - Ephesians 5:1,2

We have another problem here with the artificial chapter division. This verse is supposed to run straight through from the last verse of the previous chapter, which says:

> *"Be kind to one another, tender-hearted, forgiving one another, as God in Christ forgave you."*
>
> - Ephesians 4:32

This verse highlights the motive for imitating God: as God in Christ forgave you. The initiative of forgiveness here is in God. Out of that precedent we are exhorted to imitate God. In fact, this imitation of God in sacrifice towards others can be understood on the basis of the superlative revelation of the whole book of Ephesians.

INCARNATIONAL OFFERING OF GIFTS

In New Covenant Christianity, the direction of all gift and all offering comes first and foremost from the Father, through the Son, and the Spirit. What is more, gifts and offerings are to flow within the Body of Christ as a movement from God so that His profligate generosity might overflow. Again, there are numerous biblical examples of this.

> *"I have received full payment and more. I am well supplied, having received from Epaphroditus the gifts you sent, a fragrant offering, a sacrifice acceptable and pleasing to God. And my God will supply every need of yours according to his riches in glory in Christ Jesus."*
>
> - PHILIPPIANS 4:18,19

It is evident that the offering and sacrifice which proved

acceptable and pleasing to God was the gift from the Philippians to Paul. Their sacrificial gift was to be the channel for God to supply the material needs of Paul. Paul then confidently assures them that what they have given will be reimbursed abundantly by the Giver.

Paul writes in Ephesians:

> *"Be kind to one another, tender-hearted, forgiving one another, as God in Christ forgave you. Therefore be imitators of God, as beloved children. And walk in love, as Christ loved us and gave Himself up for us, a fragrant offering and sacrifice to God."*
>
> *- Ephesians 4:32 - 5:2*

Christ's sacrifice to God is to love *us*. The point here is that God is the primary mover. In Christ, He forgave us. Christ's sacrifice was to give Himself up for us in love. This was not confined to His death on the cross, it was outworked in His life. His life and death were a manifestation and a dissemination of the Father's compassion.

> *"As you come to him, a living stone rejected by men but in the sight of God chosen and precious, you yourselves like living stones are being built*

up as a spiritual house, to be a holy priesthood, to offer spiritual sacrifices acceptable to God through Jesus Christ."

- 1 PETER 2: 4,5

If we read 1 Peter 2:5 in isolation, we may well draw the conclusion that these "spiritual sacrifices acceptable to God" are sacrifices of service out of a need to become accepted by Him. But it would be a mistake to assume this because we are *already* accepted by God in His Beloved Son. The spiritual sacrifices that God finds acceptable are those which are "through Jesus Christ." They are not a standard to be attained but rather an alignment with His heart. They are sacrifices which maintain the bond of love among the Father's family (1 Peter 1:14).

1 Peter 1:22 identifies the essential elements of these acceptable sacrifices as:

"...a sincere brotherly love, loving one another earnestly from a pure heart."

The sacrifice that is acceptable to God is the 'sincere brotherly love...earnestly from a pure heart." Familial love flows out of filial love which has its vitality in the Source of love. To love brothers and sisters there must be a consciousness that we are bound together by the ties of sharing in Christ's sonship to the Father. It is the love of parents which bind the family together, and incites love among siblings. Vertical love from parent to child is the precursor and motivator of horizontal love.

God is spirit. He reveals and manifests Himself in human flesh. The point of incarnation is that Spirit is able to be clothed in human flesh. Jesus demonstrated this and now the Body of Christ is the incarnation of God on earth. If we don't function freely as the incarnate Body of Christ, then the love of the Father will be hindered from flowing as He wants it to. The more we are filled with the Father's love, the more it will overflow and be demonstrated through our human personalities.

The following biblical texts relate specifically to gifts. These verses show unequivocally that the direction of gift-giving comes from heaven:

> *"Every good gift and every perfect gift is from above,*
> *coming down from the Father of lights with whom*
> *there is no variation or shadow due to change."*
>
> - JAMES 1:17

> *"When He ascended on high, He led a host of*

captives and He gave gifts to men.”

> *- Ephesians 4:8*

“For the wages of sin is death but the gift of God is eternal life in Christ Jesus our Lord.”

> *- Romans 6:23*

“And God is able to make all grace abound to you, so that having all sufficiency in all things at all times, you may abound in every good work. As it is written,

“He has distributed freely, he has given to the poor; his righteousness endures forever.”

He who supplies seed to the sower and bread for food will supply and multiply your seed for sowing and increase the harvest of your righteousness. You will be enriched in every way to be generous in every way, which through us will produce thanksgiving to God. For the ministry of this service is not only supplying the needs of the saints but is also overflowing in many thanksgivings to God...Thanks be to God for his inexpressible gift!”

> *- 2 Corinthians 9: 8-15*

The seed is thrown liberally from the hand of the Sower. The seed is dropped from heaven. It is dispensed so that it can be distributed on earth. Ministry is the distribution of the gift from heaven.

New Covenant gift-giving comes from being totally accepted by God and is focused towards others. The only sacrifice, offering and gift that goes to God is a response of thankfulness and praise.

In all of the examples I have mentioned, the direction of the gift, the offering and the sacrifice is from heaven to earth, from God to us. And we are co-participants in that as we give gifts, offerings and sacrifices from God to those more vulnerable than us in status, authority or resources.

"For I was hungry and you gave me food. I was thirsty and you gave me drink. I was a stranger and you welcomed me. I was naked and you clothed me. I was sick and you visited me. I was in prison and you came to me...Truly I say to you, as you did to the least of these my brothers, you did it to me."

- MATTHEW 25:35,36, 40

To speak and act for the famine-stricken, the refugee, the marginalised, the infirm, and the condemned is to do so for God Himself. God's sacrificial love invariably flows to the lowest and weakest place. (SEE DIAGRAM 6)

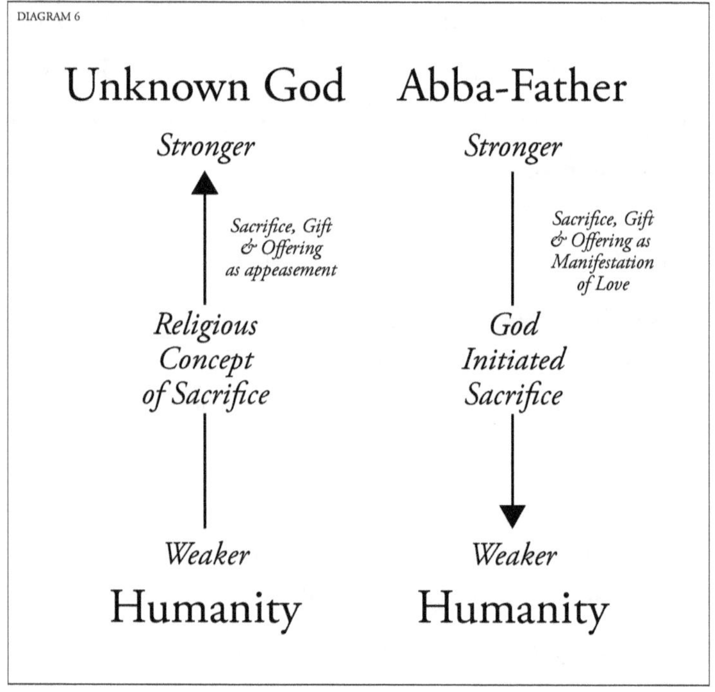

MINISTRY IN A DOWNWARD DIRECTION

A lot of Christian service and ministry is based on a religious concept of sacrifice. Many try to serve God out of their human strength to impress Him and earn His blessing, but this inevitably leads to collapse and burnout. Paul understood that ministry was the exact opposite of this. He saw himself as the steward of a great treasure of boundless capacity and priceless worth. That treasure was available for him to distribute freely wherever he could.

If we are ever pressured to sacrifice for someone who is stronger, more equipped, of higher status, or having more resources than we have, this is spiritual abuse. Jesus warned the disciples against this:

> *"You know that the rulers of the Gentiles lord it over them, and their great ones exercise authority over them. It shall not be so among you. But whoever would be great among you must be your servant, and whoever would be first among you must be your slave, even as the Son of Man came not to be served but to serve, and to give his life as a ransom for many."*
>
> *- MATTHEW 20:25-28*

A truly biblical style of leadership lays down its life for the flock. Lording it over others only occurs when the arrow is pointing upward to achieve a standard. True Christian authority is gained in serving, in taking the towel and the basin to minister to others.

The apostle Paul exemplified this attitude in his relationship to the communities that he founded. He treated them as a parent treats beloved children. Here is what he writes in 2 Corinthians 12:

> *"Here for the third time I am ready to come to you. And I will not be a burden, for I seek not what is yours but you. For children are not bound to save up for their parents, but parents for their children. I will most gladly spend and be spent for your souls."*
>
> - 2 CORINTHIANS 12:14-15

New Covenant ministry is the manifestation and pouring out of the love of God. The priestly ministry of sonship serves at the altar by offering life *from* God as a living sacrifice - not by offering the sacraments *to* God. The son, in a priestly function, takes the bread from heaven, the life of God, and distributes it to those who long to partake of that life. The hungry are given a piece of the Living Bread that comes out of heaven. They are sustained and strengthened by that Bread. They are offered the sacrament of the New Wine. This wine of the outpoured love of the Father gladdens the heart and sends an inner fire through the breast to bring warmth and cheer.

One of the things that liberated me, after a lifetime of sacrifice on the upward trajectory to please God, was to come to the realisation that I cannot give what I don't already have. Throughout my life I had tried to give something that I didn't possess. I was giving in order to gain what I was seeking - acceptance and approval. My sacrifice was an offering from a cup that was draining out and that eventually became empty. In contrast to this, Christianity is giving out of the overflow of what we already receive in never-ending bounty.

I once was a priest, appointed from among men. I wasn't literally ordained by a denomination but I spent a lot of time making sacrifices for sin, mine and others. Now I am a "minister of the New Covenant" (2 Corinthians 3:6) on the other side of the equation. I minister the flow of love streaming downwards from the Father. The sacrament that I distribute is the substance of the Father's love. My humanity, in all its weakness and brokenness, has become the altar upon which the sacrifice of the life of God is presented so that others can receive it.

CHAPTER SEVEN

The Beams of Love

~

"And we are put on earth a little space, That we may learn to bear the beams of love."

- WILLIAM BLAKE

"Love, in fact, is the vocation which includes all others. It is a universe of its own, comprising all time and space. It is eternal."

-THERESE OF LISIEUX

A Christianity that flows out of the Father's love has a completely different character to the Christianity that we have previously experienced. A Christianity that is not energised by the love of God leaves us languishing in the Old Covenant and in religion. A Christianity sourced in the Father brings us into union with Jesus and we enter the New Covenant of sonship. We are co-inheritors with Jesus of the promise of the Father.

What He has been given in His sonship has become ours, and the purpose of our life is to explore this in faith.

True Christianity brings us, with Jesus, into the bosom of the Father. As we receive the Father's love, we are coming increasingly into the experience of being "in the Beloved." When we are united with Christ, He is focusing on the Father and we are caught up into the relationship that Jesus has with the Father. The whole point of Christianity is to be united with Christ and to be one with Him in His filial relationship to the Father. God intends that we are to live in Christ, united with Christ, caught up in His receiving of His Father's love and reciprocating that love back to the Father. We are not talking about different loves here. It is the same substance, the same love, sourced in the Father, expressed and reciprocated by the Son, and shed abroad in us by the Holy Spirit.

For this to be made real in our own lives something is needed on our side. What is required of us when we realise that we have been on this self-induced quest to become like God? What happens now that we realise that we are caught in the upward movement of religion? First of all, we need to *repent*.

NON-RELIGIOUS REPENTANCE

The word 'repentance' is used often in Christian meetings. It is a word favoured by religious preachers. Some of us cannot help tensing up a little when we are called to repent, and that is understandable. We relate it to continual failure and an endless cycle of condemnation.

Repentance (Greek: *metanoia*), however, simply means "a change of direction." It doesn't mean making a mental assent to a different set of beliefs, but a change in the direction of the heart. It means crossing over from being an achiever to being a receiver, crossing from the upward movement of religion to the downward movement of the Father's love.

Most repentance within Christianity is done on the left-hand side of my diagram. When we fail to ascend high enough and fall into some moral failure, we 'repent' and then try and climb up the ascent again. We stay in the upward movement. For many of us, Christianity has become like a game of Snakes and Ladders; as we move from the start to the finish, sometimes we land on a ladder and move upwards closer to God but then we can land on a snake and slip back towards the start. We are caught in a constant cycle of repentance, going to the 'altar' one more time, and never moving beyond that. Our repentance keeps us enmeshed within the web of the Tree of the Knowledge of Good and Evil. We are trapped in the repetitive cycle of guilt, remorse and striving to become better. (SEE DIAGRAM 7)

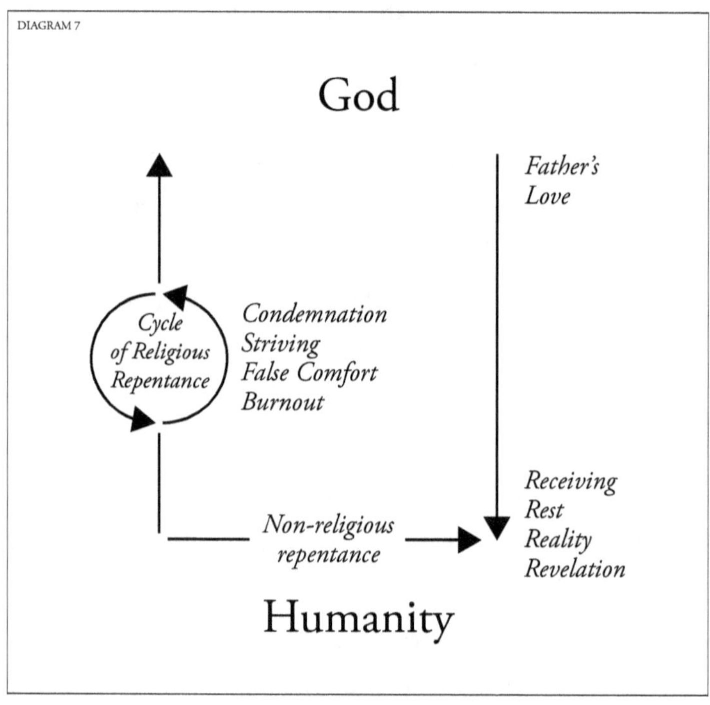

Repentance is not saying sorry out of remorse, and then striving in our own strength to do better again. Repentance is simply a switch from the upward-reaching side to the downward-receiving side. For a receiver of grace, there is no attempt to climb higher. It doesn't matter how low you are. In fact, the lower you descend, the more you can receive.

Excellence in Receiving

James Jordan has commented that if a Christian has to become competent at anything, they need to become a good receiver. The better a receiver you are, the more effective your experience of Christianity will be. Christianity, in its essence, is the life and love of God. Nothing more and nothing less. The basic stance of the Christian in sonship is to become a receiver and always be a receiver. The life of heaven flows downwards to those who receive it.

This gives tremendous hope to those of us who have descended to the depths. I have discovered that no matter how messed up I am, grace flows down to that darkest place. I do not need to improve myself or lift myself up. I simply need to open my heart to receive the grace-gift that is already flowing from God. That grace transforms me and brings me to the bosom of the Father.

When temptation comes, I have discovered that I can go to the lowest place. Instead of hiding the issue or denying it, I can admit to the temptation by being completely honest about it before the Father, and then receive the down-flow of love and grace that comes to that place of humility. Any time I return to striving, I can repent by changing direction (*metanoia*) and return to the side where Love is flowing down.

Religion seeks to achieve something, ultimately the acceptance of God. Sonship Christianity, however, receives the love of God. I recall someone saying that the end of all theology and the goal to which all the mystics of the Church attained was to experience resting in the arms of the Father. When we get our eyes opened to see His purpose from the very beginning, there is no longer any need to strive towards that goal. Begin to open your heart where you are today, even a tiny crack, and receive the Father's love for you.

COMFORTING REST

This revelation brings us into rest. When we are at the bottom of the downward movement, we are lying down and receiving everything that comes to us. I am permanently burned out with the striving spirituality of seeking God and trying to please Him in the upward direction. Rest can only come when we are comforted by the mothering love of God our Father.

Comfort and nurture reside intrinsically in the heart of the Father. It is important to know that comfort was not introduced as a response to orphan-ness. Comfort preceded the comfortless state of orphan-ness. The orphan state is a state of departure from the original comfort in the presence of the Father. We may have been born into this comfortless existence of the fallen condition but the place of comfort is *there already* in God.

Prior to anything going wrong in the cosmic order, the Trinity lived in a habitat of comfort with one another. The life of the Godhead is a life enveloped in the comfort of home. The only-begotten Son, who is in the bosom of the Father, lives eternally in that place. Eternally begotten of the Father, of the same substance, yet eternally generated from the Father, the Son is always surrounded by the Father's enclosing nurture. Within the mystery of the Trinitarian life of God, the Second Person of the Godhead lives within the bosom of the First Person of the Godhead. The Holy Spirit is the purveyor of the Father's comfort.

The fall of Lucifer did not dislodge anything in the life of the Trinity. Comfort was a pre-existing quality of the life of God. The motherly traits of the heart of God, which the feminine aspect of His image expresses, are an essential aspect of His nature. It is important to understand that the paternal and maternal descriptions of God's nature are *not* metaphorical, they are *literal.* In other words, fatherhood and motherhood begin in God.

Becoming assured of this truth, we gain more and more confidence in our unassailable place in the affections of the Father. At last we can relax and find rest for our souls. All activity and fruitfulness then comes from that place of rest.

FINDING CONFIDENCE IN REALITY

Jesus says, in John 8:32, "...and you will know the truth, and the truth will set you free." Truth is not having correct doctrine, which is what many believe it to be. Truth is ultimate reality. To be set free by truth is to be set free by reality. I am becoming increasingly free by living in reality. In this place, I can embrace the reality of my incompetence, my weakness, my vulnerability to temptation. Reality is a state of integration with our own humanity.

In religion, when we see ourselves for who we really are, we are continually under condemnation. In a life lived in the Father's love, however, we can fully admit our weakness, our vulnerability to temptation, and our total inability to improve ourselves, knowing we can ask the Father to help us, because we know that He loves us unconditionally. His flow of grace will bring a substance of peace to the soul, and temptation will fall away. My strategy when faced with temptation is not to rise up and attempt to overcome it by my own willpower. Rather, I lie down under it and let the Father rescue me. When I am faced with temptation, I face it with honesty, admitting that part of me *really desires* to do what I am tempted to do, then love can come to my place of honesty. I find every time that grace flows to the lowest place.

The writer and contemplative Thomas Merton made the following incisive observation:

> *"Perhaps the reason why so few men believe in God is that they have ceased to believe that even God can love them. The man who is not afraid to admit everything that he sees to be wrong with himself, and yet recognises that he may be the object of God's love precisely because of his shortcomings, can begin to be sincere. His sincerity is based on confidence, not in his illusions about himself, but in the endless, unfailing mercy of God."*[7]

---

7. T. P. McDonnell (Ed.), *A Thomas Merton Reader*, New York, 1989.

Positioned for Ongoing Revelation

One of the most exciting and precious discoveries that we experience at the bottom of the downward movement of the Father's love is that supernatural revelation flows. There can *never* be revelation on the striving, upward movement. Revelation flows on the side of resting and receiving. Revelation flows to babes, *not to* the wise and prudent (Matthew 11:25). There is a crying need today for revelation, for God's insight into everything. The reason why revelation is so rare is because the upward striving of religion is so prevalent. The prelude to revelation is relaxation!

Don't be afraid to descend into your own brokenness and face your deep need, because revelation flows there.

This book is about foundations. It is about removing the foundations of religion and revealing the true foundations of Christianity. The love of God the Father is the starting point of all that is Christianity. The first principle in the Christian life, in *all* life, is that *God is Love*.

In contemporary Christianity, there is an abundance of rhetoric about our love for God, but we experience very little of God's love for us. I used to love God intensely, but I then came to a stunning realisation:

If we love God more than we have a revelation of His love for us, it is merely a religious affection.

God can only be truly loved in response. He can only be loved with the love that He has already poured into our hearts.

The following quote by Raniero Cantalamessa articulates the deep-seated problem that Christendom is faced with:

> *"We have a tendency to put first the duty of us loving God, rather than the primary fact of God loving us first: "But revelation gives more importance to the second meaning; to God's love for us rather than to our love for God. Aristotle said that God moves the world in so far as he is loved, that is, in so far as he is the object of love and the final cause of all its creatures; but the Bible says the exact opposite, that God creates and moves the world in so far as he loves the world. Concerning God's love, therefore, the most important thing is not that man should love God but that God loves man and that he loved him first...Everything else depends on this including our own chance of loving God."*[8]

---

8. Quotation taken from Ralph Martin, *Does God Really Love Me?*, Ann Arbor, 1995.

The whole point of this book is that we can relax and enter into the flow of God's initiative and God's life-energy. When we give up our own initiative in Christianity, we will discover that God always has, and always will, take the initiative. Our part is to receive and respond to that divine initiative.

The Christian life is not to be our own self-motivated life; it is to be a yielding to the life of God within us. We only learn to yield to resurrection life through our own death and brokenness and giving up our religious effort to please God. The life of the Trinity is a life of rest and peace, security and joy. It does not have concerns about its future survival but exults in the eternal *now*. God's world is exuberant and extravagant. The atmosphere and vibrancy of that world is the Father's love. His love holds the universe together.

The Christianity that I lived for most of my life, a radically obedient and devoted Christianity, came to an abrupt end. A set of circumstances exposed my spirituality for what it really was, merely a system of belief and practice devoid of any interior comfort or experience of the love of God. Through a period of extreme stress culminating in a moral failure, I came to the shocking conclusion that my sophisticated belief system had no power to actually heal my wounded and shrivelled heart.

By the grace of God, in the midst of my personal shipwreck, I was swallowed by a proverbial whale, and vomited out onto dry land. That 'dry land' happened to be a little island off the coast of Auckland, New Zealand. There I met the One whom Jesus called 'Abba' - God the Father. In a paradigm-shifting revelation and through personal encounters, I received the substance of His love and comfort into my innermost being. What is more, this revelation and the life that flows from it has become the new foundation of my life. It is a foundation not based in me at all. It is a foundation that is rooted in the eternal purpose of God, a foundation of being *already* "holy and blameless before Him in love."

When I came to the end of servant-hearted Christianity, it felt like I was walking through a thick, dark forest which became more and more overgrown until I could go no further. Then, through my tears, I saw in the undergrowth a hidden door which led the way out of the old world of Christianity of servanthood and striving into sonship and rest. That door was my admission that I had utterly failed in my own attempts to become like God. When I finally admitted that, God was able to enter my heart and show me His love.

My parting words to you, the reader, are these: Do not try to be 'a Christian' anymore. Don't try to live the Christian life. Allow God to enter into your humanness and live His life through you. Your humanity is God's dream home. God has always longed to indwell you.

William Blake penned the lines:

> *"And we are put on earth a little space, That we*
> *may learn to bear the beams of love."*

Lie down, relax and receive the beams of the Father's love!

More Books

This little book is about taking the next steps after transition, helping us explore our freedom as sons and daughters. It will open our eyes to see opportunity and expression all around us, in the exciting and in the mundane.

Available from:
www/fatherheart.net/store/books

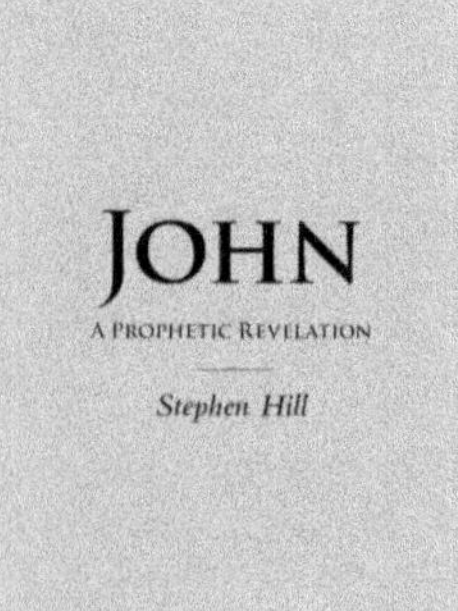

Stephen Hill's commentary on the Gospel of John is rich with prophetic insight on the Father's love. In it, he expands our understanding of Trinitarian Love and its role in creation, incarnation, sanctification and ultimately its cosmic ramifications.

Available from:
www/fatherheart.net/store/books

In this book Stephen Hill brings a freshness and revelatory interpretation of this magnificent and all-important letter of the Apostle Paul and contributes to the opening of our eyes.

Available from:
www/fatherheart.net/store/books

by Stephen Hill

This book is straight fire. God just breathes on every part of it." "I think I've never read any book which is at the same time so full of revelation and also encouraging and freeing!

Available from:
www/fatherheart.net/store/books

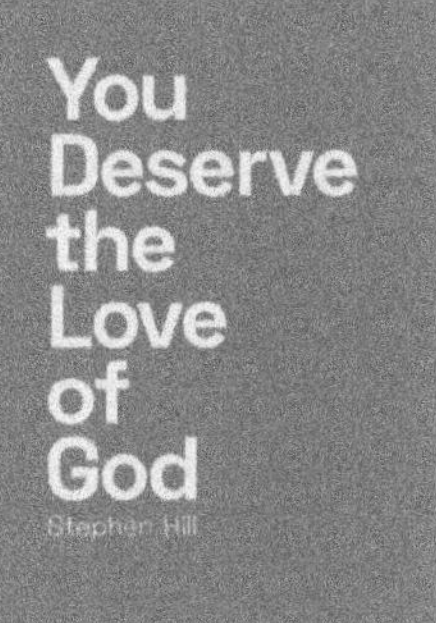

This book is about what God believes about us, the human race. The truth is, we cannot experience the love of God outside our humanity. You and I are the highest point of God's purposes, the apex of God's creation.

Available from:
www/fatherheart.net/store/books